LEADING WORSHIP FOR WORKERS

How to Design Liturgies for All of Life

Matthew Kaemingk and Kathryn Roelofs

Baker Academic
a division of Baker Publishing Group
Grand Rapids, Michigan

© 2026 by Matthew Kaemingk and Kathryn Roelofs

Published by Baker Academic
a division of Baker Publishing Group
Grand Rapids, Michigan
BakerAcademic.com

Printed in the United States of America

Library of Congress Cataloging-in-Publication Data
Names: Kaemingk, Matthew, 1981– author | Roelofs, Kathryn author
Title: Leading worship for workers : how to design liturgies for all of life / Matthew Kaemingk and Kathryn Roelofs.
Description: Grand Rapids, Michigan : Baker Academic, a division of Baker Publishing Group, [2026]
Identifiers: LCCN 2025027329 | ISBN 9781540969842 paperback | ISBN 9781540970022 casebound | ISBN 9781493453375 ebook | ISBN 9781493453382 pdf
Subjects: LCSH: Worship programs | Work—Religious aspects—Christianity | Employees—Religious life | Christian leadership
Classification: LCC BV198 .K34 2026
LC record available at https://lccn.loc.gov/2025027329

Cover illustration by Brittany Fan

Baker Publishing Group publications use paper produced from sustainable forestry practices and postconsumer waste whenever possible.

26 27 28 29 30 31 32   7 6 5 4 3 2 1

"Get ready to laugh, cry, and have your theology and actions formed and transformed by this excellent book! Kaemingk and Roelofs offer robust biblical and historical support for the integration of work and worship. This collaborative book not only guides readers to create original contextualized worship practices but also includes an abundant variety of resources for immediate use. A much-needed guide for all churches."

—**Amy F. Davis Abdallah**, professor, pilgrimage leader, founder and director of
Woman: A Rite of Passage, and author of *Meaning in the Moment*
and *The Book of Womanhood*

"Kaemingk and Roelofs narrow the perilous Sunday to Monday gap between worship and work by providing rich theological reflection as well as helpful and creative practices for any gathered worship experience. Whatever your ecclesial context, I am confident imaginations will be sparked, creativity unleashed, beauty indwelled, and the gathered worship experience wonderfully transformed. Imagine what it would look like if every follower of Jesus was encouraged to bring their work world into their church experience. This excellent book is a great contribution for church leaders and all who love the church to more fully embrace an integral gospel that shapes all of life. I highly recommend it!"

—**Tom Nelson**, senior pastor, Christ Community Church, Kansas City;
founder and executive chairman, Made to Flourish

"Simply brilliant. And brilliantly simple. This generous, biblically astute, imagination-expanding, and liberatingly practical book is a tour de force. It offers worship leaders and pastors a life-stage approach to integrating a congregation's daily work—at home and on the job—into every aspect of gathered worship. Rooted in a deep appreciation of the challenges of contemporary work, it brims with inspiring examples and a joyous call to creative experiment. Bravo!"

—**Mark Greene**, author of *Thank God It's Monday*; former executive director,
London Institute for Contemporary Christianity

"A unique theological handbook on how to minister to all who work and toil. Kaemingk and Roelofs encourage worship leaders to invite people to come as they truly are. What a relief! With service ideas, liturgies, prayers, songs, and more, this book is practical, useful, and hospitable."

—**Rachel Wilhelm**, worship leader, singer-songwriter,
and vice president of United Adoration

"This book offers instructive, practical wisdom for shaping worship in local congregations, parishes, campus ministries, and other ministry contexts in ways that make seamless connections between what we do together in gathered worship and how we live and serve in the workaday world. Even as the authors present many ready-to-use resources, they are also patiently and creatively teaching us how to perceive, celebrate, and pray for the work of the Holy Spirit in and through God's people in a wide array of pursuits. This is a book with transformative potential for worship ministries in a variety of circumstances."

—**John D. Witvliet**, Belmont University; senior consultant,
Calvin Institute of Christian Worship

"A valuable resource for every worship leader who seeks to help extend worship beyond the walls of the church. Offering both theological reflection and practical tools, this book can help you cultivate a gathering that invites people to bring their whole lives to God in worship and sends them back into the world to join God's mission in the world through their work."

—**Matt Rusten**, president, Made to Flourish

"Our congregations are filled with workers, yet our liturgies, songs, and prayers often lack the imagination to engage them fully. Kaemingk and Roelofs penned this handbook for all of us: ordained or lay, seasoned Christian or occasional practitioner. They invite us to honor our working identities in worship rather than checking them at the door. *Leading Worship for Workers* is practical. It is theological. And when practiced, it is transformational."

—**Nelson Cowan**, Center for Worship and the Arts, Samford University

"Connecting worship and work is not solely a topic for a Labor Day service; it is a way of life. Kaemingk and Roelofs assist local congregations by providing a rich resource for worship architects who wish to help worshipers traverse the border between daily occupation and Lord's Day worship. This is a handbook filled with biblically grounded, practical examples and exercises that help address the persisting bifurcation between the sacred and the secular."

—**Constance M. Cherry**, Robert E. Webber Institute for Worship Studies; Indiana Wesleyan University (emeritus)

"A timely and needed call to break the habit of telling worshipers, implicitly or explicitly, to leave parts of themselves behind when they enter the sanctuary. Kaemingk and Roelofs compel leaders to see, know, and love the people who come together for corporate worship as whole people. They remind us that congregants gather to worship a God who has been present with them throughout the week. The insights and suggestions in *Leading Worship for Workers* are wonderfully grounded in the realities of local church life. Refreshingly practical, this book offers words and rhythms for liturgies that affirm the value, difficulty, and dignity of labor."

—**Kelsey Kramer McGinnis**, worship correspondent, *Christianity Today*

"A much-needed resource for helping the church reclaim a robust theology of work in its weekly liturgies. With theological depth and practical tools, Kaemingk and Roelofs offer worship leaders a vision for integrating Monday through Friday into Sunday mornings. This book reminds us that God cares deeply about the work done in office buildings, in classrooms, at construction sites, and at kitchen tables—and worship should reflect that truth. A powerful guide for anyone longing to see every square inch of life brought under the lordship of Jesus Christ."

—**Jordan Raynor**, bestselling author of *The Sacredness of Secular Work*

For John Witvliet,
our colleague, mentor, and friend

Contents

Part 3: How to Bless Workers' Callings

Part 4: Creative Ideas for Deeper Engagement

Preface

As your authors, we come to the topic of work and worship from very different angles. Matthew Kaemingk is a theologian who researches the place of workers in Scripture, church history, and the global mission of the church. In addition to this theological research, Matthew has served on the ground as a "pastor to professionals" in a couple of different marketplace ministries in New York, Seattle, and Houston.

Katie Roelofs is a worship leader, pastor, and consultant who has planned and led worship for congregations in Washington, DC, for two decades. Through God's prompting and providence, this book has been simmering in our hearts and minds for a number of years now. The urgent importance of connecting work and worship was a lesson Katie learned through her experience leading worship in the nation's capital.

Washington is filled with ambitious urban professionals, politicians, and federal workers, whose work experience and identity are of central importance. Katie quickly learned that DC workers entered the sanctuary carrying a lot of . . . "stuff" from their week at work. If the songs, prayers, and blessings did not connect with all this "stuff," these workers would head back to the Hill feeling alone and spiritually empty-handed. In her current role as a worship consultant, Katie works directly with pastors and worship leaders who face similar challenges in their unique contexts and seek to cultivate liturgical practices that speak holistically to the daily lives of their people. It turns out that workers in DC are not the only ones who carry the burdens of their weeks into worship.

Ten years ago, Matthew was working on the other side of the country in the Pacific Northwest, leading a marketplace ministry with ten churches in the greater Seattle area. It was a rainy January morning and Matthew was busy planning a weekend retreat on "faith and work" with his colleague Cory Willson. Being academics, their original plan was to give a series of intellectual lectures on a biblical perspective of work.

However, as they began to plan the retreat, Cory and Matthew had a change of heart. They decided that these workers didn't need a lecture on faith and work; *they needed to actually practice it*. They wanted to create a worshipful space in which these men and women could carry their workplace joys and heartbreaks directly to God. They wanted to offer these workers some more contemplative moments of prayer, song, and silence to reflect on the work of their hands in the presence of God.

To their utter disappointment, Cory and Matthew found almost no songs or worship resources that could help them plan or lead worship for workers. This gap haunted them.

Being theologians, they set about doing what theologians do—they started a research project. After three years of intense biblical and historical research, they did another thing theologians do. They wrote a book.

Published in 2020, *Work and Worship: Reconnecting Our Labor and Liturgy* explores the modern divorce between work and worship and provides a detailed biblical case for why our worship services urgently need to reengage the work of everyday Christians. While Cory and Matthew are proud of this book, it left something important undone. Although it explains *why* the reconnection between worship and work matters, it does not fully explain *how* churches can practically accomplish this in the modern world. This is why Matthew and Katie wrote this guide. It offers leaders the practical tools, ideas, and resources they need to actually plan and lead worship for workers.

Now that you have some background about us and the origin story behind this book, we turn to who we most hope to reach. This book is intended for all pastors, worship leaders, and worship teams who want their worship services to deeply engage the lives of workers.

Regardless of your worship style or denomination, this book is for you. Whether you are Baptist or Brethren, Charismatic or Catholic, you will discover new ideas and practices for engaging workers that can be adapted to your unique approach to worship. The same goes for congregations that are predominantly urban or rural, young or old, white collar or blue. We acknowledge that some of our suggestions will not be a fit with your particular congregation. Our deep hope is that these practices fuel your creativity to adapt and reimagine them for your people and worship.

As an example, if your church is more spontaneous and informal in its approach to prayer, you can feel free to take our more formal and written prayers and spontaneously "riff" off of their content. Like a good jazz player, pick up the basic beat that we are laying down and make it your own. *We have no desire to change your style of worship. Our goal is to help your unique style connect in a deeper way with workers.*

This book is for everyone. The human longing to offer the work of our hands to God in worship is culturally and denominationally universal. In every time and every place, human beings have lifted up their work and asked God to heal, protect, and bless it.

While we are from North America, we've found that some of the most exciting examples of work and worship today are being developed by Christians in Africa, Asia, and Latin America. We've learned much from their witness. Similarly, while we come from the Reformed tradition, we have greatly benefited from collaborating with a wide range of traditions on these matters, from Pentecostals to Lutherans, from Anglicans to Methodists. Moreover, while we are Protestants, our historical research has clearly revealed that our Roman Catholic and Orthodox friends have been thinking about these issues of work and worship for much longer than we have. Many of the "new" and "creative" resources you will find in this book draw on their older and deeper wells.

One final note before we proceed. In addition to the book you hold in your hands, we have also launched a web resource called worshipforworkers.com. On this website you will find a wealth of worship resources that we could not fit into the pages of this book. This is a dynamic and growing website. Every month songwriters, pastors, workers, artists, and liturgists from all over the world are contributing original songs, prayers, and blessings that are free for you to adapt and use in your congregation. As you read this book, please feel welcome to visit this website and sample our library of resources and ideas.

PART 1

WHERE DO WE START?

1

Why Do We Need Worship for Workers?

"So, what do you do for a living?"

Whenever we meet someone new, it's one of the first questions asked. The reason, of course, is quite simple. What we do is important to us. On average, people spend a third of their lives working. Because work takes up so much mental, physical, and emotional space, it should be no surprise that it is absolutely central to our sense of identity and purpose. When our heads hit the pillow at night and when we get up in the morning, our minds and hearts often drift to the things of work.

Given the centrality of work, it should be no surprise that some of our biggest spiritual questions, longings, and frustrations are directly connected to our various careers and callings. *God, why do I have to navigate working for this boss? God, do you see and hear what I'm dealing with? God, should I change careers? Where am I called? What should I do? I'm suffering at work, do you see me?*

The fact that work plays an enormous role in shaping our identity is not surprising. What *is* surprising is that—despite work's massive importance in our lives—modern worship services are almost completely silent on the matter. Gathered together in the sanctuary, workers will hear almost nothing about one of the most consuming things they've been doing all week long. The songs and sermons, confessions and communion, blessings and benedictions remain curiously silent on the topic of work.

Given this silence, it should come as no surprise that a deep and growing chasm has opened up in people's minds and hearts between their faith and their work. This yawning gap between Sunday worship and Monday work has had a devastating effect on both sides of the equation. Our worship feels increasingly detached, abstract, and irrelevant to our daily lives. Our work, on the other hand, becomes devoid of spiritual meaning and purpose, increasingly isolated from the power and presence of God. When we live in two separate pieces, work here and worship over there, both sides—not surprisingly—begin to suffer.

This book is designed for pastors and worship leaders who recognize this problem in their own congregations and, more importantly, want to change it.

In the pages that follow, we invite leaders to a place of curiosity and imagination where they can begin to craft worship services that speak directly to the realities the workers in their congregation face throughout the week. Through creative exercises, practical examples, and a rich selection of resources, leaders can begin to dream about how to lead worship that engages the lives and longings of workers.

As this is a handbook, we are largely concerned with the question of *how*. *How* can we effectively lead worship for workers? That said, in this first chapter we need to briefly discuss our *why*. *Why* should pastors and worship leaders even care about work and workers? *Why* should the "secular" world of work even be addressed in the "sacred" world of worship?

In this introductory chapter, we will also tackle a few frequently asked questions and direct challenges that we often encounter when discussing worship for workers. People have asked us, "Who counts as a worker?" What about stay-at-home parents, the retired, the unemployed, and children? Doesn't an emphasis on "workers" exclude people? More than that, my identity is in Christ, not in my work. Christ alone should be the focus of worship—not work. Right? But more than that, I'm not just a "worker." I have many callings; I'm a parent, a spouse, a neighbor, a friend, a citizen, a volunteer, and much more. Why all this emphasis on work?

Finally, isn't this just another flash in the pan worship fad? Won't "worship for workers" eventually die the same death as every other modern worship trend that preceded it?

We obviously have a lot to get to, so let's get started.

Theological Commitments

While this book is open to a wide variety of worship styles and cultural contexts, it is narrow in one very specific respect. We are rather inflexible in our theological commitment to workers and their place within the mission of God and the worship of the church. Our (somewhat monomaniacal) focus on work and worship emerges from five theological commitments.

God Cares About Workers

God hears the cries of workers. He knows their hearts and wants them to be treated justly. God delights in their victories, care, and craftsmanship. God accepts their firstfruits with joy. Each and every person is seen and loved by God as they go about their daily calling. This book assumes that if the God of the universe cares about workers, the church should as well. Likewise, if God maintains a posture of care and curiosity toward these men, women, and children, our worship services should reflect this same divine posture.

God Cares About Workplaces

The workplace is a primary space in which followers of Jesus will fulfill every major command found in Scripture. Through our daily work we steward, order, and fill creation. Through our work we love and serve our neighbor. Through our work we learn to follow Christ, grow in the Spirit, and share the gospel. We don't need to urgently find a mission trip in order to serve. The Great Commission, the great commandment, and the cultural mandate can all be honored in and through our daily work. Lord willing, the workplace can be the stage on which the mission of God is played out. As Steven Garber writes, the workplace is absolutely central, not incidental, to the mission of God in the world.[1] Work and workplaces matter to God. He sees and cares about them. When church leaders accept these theological truths, they begin to ask disruptive questions: If God cares about workers, shouldn't our church? If workplaces are central to the mission of God, shouldn't they be central to the mission of our church as well?

---

1. Steven Garber, *The Seamless Life: A Tapestry of Love and Learning, Worship and Work* (InterVarsity, 2020).

God Wants Two Kinds of Worship, Not One

God delights when his people gather together to worship in the sanctuary through song and praise. God *also* delights when his people scatter out into the city to worship his name through their daily work and service. Whether gathered or scattered, both forms of worship matter to God. One cannot say, "I went to church, so I'm done worshiping for the week." In the same way, one cannot say, "I worship God through my work, so I don't need to gather with God's people for worship." These two kinds of worship actually depend on each other, and neither can replace the other. In this book, our definition of *worship* is always twofold: Gathering on Sunday morning is a singular moment of worship, and it is the launching pad for a whole week of scattered worship. Whether God's beloved are gathered or scattered, the glory of God is a people worshiping and working in his name.

God Wants Worship to Be a Dialogue

Worship is not merely "an experience," a form of entertainment or education. Worshipers are not submissive consumers of content. Worship is a dynamic and active conversation between a people and their God. As such, worshipers enter the sanctuary to actively participate and contribute to a divine dialogue.

In the Old Testament, worship was not something the people of Israel "experienced"; it was something they *did*. They actively prepared and entered worship ready to offer the work of their hands to God and say something to him about where that work came from (Deut. 26). Their songbook (the Psalter) illustrates the many diverse things a worker could say to God during worship. Israelite farmers and merchants were invited to carry their workplace laments and confessions, their petitions and praises directly into worship. They never came to the Lord empty-handed. Instead, they actually brought the fruits of their physical labor with them directly into the sanctuary and offered it to God in praise and thanksgiving (Lev. 2; Deut. 16:16–17; 26:1–12, 14). Israelite worship was not a monologue. Both sides had something to offer and something to say (Exod. 2:23–24; 3:7; Ps. 66:16).

In the same way, worship today *must* be a dialogue, a lively back-and-forth between the people and their God. When God calls workers into worship, they need to come prepared to contribute to the conversation. Like their Israelite forebears, they never come empty-handed. They enter the sanctuary carrying their week with them. They can bring their workplace questions and confessions, laments and longings, fruits and frustrations, trusting that God will also have something to say back to them. In worship, God will offer them his holy Word, his Spirit and power, his comfort and command, and ultimately he will offer his very self to them as a holy sacrifice.

In view of these mercies, they will respond to his self-offering by offering their whole self—their careers and callings—as a living sacrifice, holy and pleasing to God (Rom. 12:1). In this, workers cannot hold back. They must offer God all the cares of their daily work—their career ambitions, their workplace concerns and relationships, all the various projects, portfolios, and deadlines that make up their daily lives. They cannot be passive consumers; they must contribute.

As a response to Christ's offering, worship cannot be a passive, abstract, or distant experience. In the sanctuary, God offers his work and we offer ours.

God Expects Sunday's Worship to Impact Monday's Work

Our private worship should have public consequences. When a worker participates in an active conversation with God, that dialogue should impact the way they enter the marketplace. When we sing songs of grace and mercy in the sanctuary, those songs should continue to resonate in the way we treat others on Monday. What are we to say about people who enter the sanctuary and assume postures of humility and contrition yet go into the office on Monday and refuse to apologize for their mistakes? Noses up, chests out, they assume a completely different posture.

In the Old Testament, this was one of the primary complaints of the prophets. Israelites were acting one way in the sanctuary and another in the marketplace. One day they would gather together to sing with loud voices about God's justice and mercy. The next day they would lie, cheat, and oppress their coworkers without a trace of justice or mercy (Isa. 58:1–14; Amos 5:21–23; 8:1–12). If we are to be people of integrity, we cannot live two lives. We cannot have divided hearts (Ps. 86:11) or "serve two masters" (Matt. 6:24). The songs and prayers of our worship commit us to a way of working in the world (Ps. 143:5, 8). As Isaiah proclaims,

> Come, let us go up to the mountain of the LORD,
>   to the temple of the God of Jacob.

> He will teach us his ways,
> so that we may walk in his paths. (Isa. 2:3)

If our daily work does not reflect the grace and mercy of our worship, something has gone terribly wrong. Our gracious dialogue with God on Sunday should recruit us for gracious dialogues with coworkers on Monday.

These five theological commitments should be neither surprising nor scandalous. They're relatively simple and straightforward. Most importantly, they are clearly evident in the witness of ancient Israel and the early church. Their biblical and historical foundations have already been thoroughly demonstrated in the exhaustive research outlined in the book *Work and Worship: Reconnecting Our Labor and Liturgy*. Yet, despite all this evidence, it's exceedingly rare to find these five theological commitments embodied in worship services today. How might we right this wrong? That is the task of this book.

Is "Worship for Workers" Just a Passing Fad?

Isn't "worship for workers" just another trend that will soon pass away? Shouldn't we keep to our historical worship traditions of largely ignoring work and workers?

Funny enough, historical research has revealed the exact opposite to be true. Connecting work and worship is neither new nor revolutionary. In fact, it is a very old idea and, in many ways, incredibly traditional.

Adam and Eve, called to be the priests of the garden, are commanded to both work and worship in deep communion with God. They know of no division between the two activities. After leaving the garden, the first thing Cain and Abel do is present the work of their hands to God (Gen. 4). This pattern only continues. The entirety of the Old Testament is filled with this strange human activity: People constantly take the work of their hands and lift it up to God as if he cared to see it (Lev. 2; Deut. 16:16–17; 26:1–12, 14).

The nation of Israel begins with workers crying out to God about their harsh labor conditions (Exod. 2:23). The very first thing they learn about their God is that they can talk to him about their struggles at work. More than that, this unusual God immediately proves that he will listen and respond to workers in distress.

When Israel's farmers harvest their crops, they're instructed to immediately carry their produce into worship. At the altar, workers (not the priest) lead a special worship service where they declare in front of their whole town that their work belongs to God and that all glory is his alone. This worker/worship leader then hosts a feast in which they share and celebrate their firstfruits with the poor, their coworkers, and the priest (Deut. 26:1–12).

The Psalter is filled with references to farming and markets, money and cattle, rich and poor. The psalms characterize God as a shepherd and a farmer, an irrigator and an engineer, and they even invite workers to talk to God about all the liars, cheats, and bullies they encounter in the marketplace (Pss. 55:11; 62:4; 69:4; 73:3–12; 109:4). The Psalms scholar John Goldingay writes that when the people cry out, "Prosper for us the work of our hands—O prosper the work of our hands!" they mean what they say. "Hey God," they shout, "just grant that all the hard work we do in sowing and plowing, in building and planting, pays off rather than being a waste of time. Please, for your name's sake, don't let all this hard work slip away. Establish it."[2]

These patterns of connecting worship and work do not cease with the coming of Christ and the rise of the early church. The earliest documents from ancient Christianity specifically command the first Christian ministers to welcome workers and bless what they've produced. Like the ancient Israelites before them, early Christian farmers continued to carry in their firstfruits (including grapes, figs, pomegranates, olives, apples, prunes, quinces, cherries, and almonds). Urban Christians, on the other hand, brought a wide variety of handcrafted products from their kitchens, kilns, and workshops. Commercial and industrial offerings included articles of clothing, bread, currency, cheese, oil, wine, and a variety of crafts.

The *Didache*, one of the oldest and most trusted Christian texts, clearly instructs believers to carry their work into worship. Men and women, rich and poor, farmers and craftsmen, homemakers and merchants—all were to bring their offering. One of the oldest surviving pieces of art in the history of the Christian faith is a series of sanctuary mosaics that depict the earliest Christians carrying the work of their hands into worship. This offering was their *leitourgia*, the work of the people, their holy service to God and community.

---

2. John Goldingay, *Psalms*, vol. 3, *Psalms 90–150*, Baker Commentary on the Old Testament Wisdom and Psalms (Baker Academic, 2008), 34.

From the victory and donor panels in the floor mosaics at Aquileia's Basilica of Santa Maria. Assunta. Zairon / CC BY-SA 4.0 / Wikimedia Commons

Figure 1.1. A donor brings a basket of bread

The earliest worship books included prayers and liturgies to bless specific kinds of workers and products. What if a dairy farmer carries his best cheese into worship? What if someone else brings their olives? The early church knew what to do: "If anyone should offer cheese and olives, let him say thus: 'Sanctify this milk that has been coagulated, coagulating us also to our love. Make also this fruit of the olive not depart from your sweetness, which is a symbol of your richness that you have poured from the tree for life for those who hope in you.'"[3]

The historical record is clear: Early Christian worship did not facilitate a worker's *escape* from work and the world—quite the opposite. Early worship *connected* workers to the earth, their bodies, and their community. Bread and

---

3. Paul F. Bradshaw, Maxwell E. Johnson, and L. Edward Phillips, *The Apostolic Tradition: A Commentary*, ed. Harold W. Attridge, Hermeneia (Fortress, 2002), 14.

Figure 1.2. A fisherman brings an offering from his daily catch

wine, hands and feet, water and song—all these material and "worldly" elements were included, made holy, and consecrated to the Lord in worship. "For everything God created is good, and nothing is to be rejected if it is received with thanksgiving, because it is consecrated by the word of God and prayer" (1 Tim. 4:4–5). "So whether you eat or drink or whatever you do, do it all for the glory of God" (1 Cor. 10:31). For you shall love the Lord your God "with all your strength" (Mark 12:30).

This pattern of work and worship continued in the medieval church, with priests leading services with farmers in the fields, asking for God's protection from drought and pests. We also see this pattern in the ship harbors of Venice, where priests would bless the fishing and merchant vessels before they set sail on the dangerous seas. We can see it in medieval England, where, after the first grain harvest, the farmers would gather in their church and lift the first loaf from the harvest in celebration of God's work and theirs.

Figure 1.3. A woman brings clusters of grapes for the Eucharist wine

We can hear the connection between work and worship in the field spiritu-
als of the Black church. The first African Americans didn't meet Jesus in a
church building; they met him in the fields as they worked and worshiped
with their Lord amid the brutality of slavery. Never in separate boxes, their
faith and work were one.

Is work and worship just a modern fad? Exhaustive biblical and historical
evidence indicate a firm and clear no. *If anything, the new and faddish thing
is to lead worship services that ignore our work.*

Why Is Reconnecting Work and Worship So Important?

"Because the Bible says so" or "Because the early Christians did it" are, of
course, very good reasons why your worship services should engage the work

of your people. However, if the reader requires more reasons, we will oblige and offer five very practical considerations.

Missional Importance

Workers are absolutely central to the mission of your church.

Pastors cannot be everywhere in the community. They're not omnipresent. Nor are they gifted, called, or competent to run the city's restaurants, factories, software teams, or after-school programs. You don't want them performing your root canal. Pastors alone can't fulfill the mission of God throughout the local community—but the people can.

Every week missionaries fill your pews, and you don't have to raise any money to support them. Each Sunday you bless and send these workers into your schools, hospitals, neighborhoods, businesses, and nonprofits. Who knows, your church may even have secret agents working in city hall. If your service ends with nothing but "Thanks for coming! We will see you next week!" you will have missed your best opportunity to activate your church for mission. Here we see *the missional reason* your worship should engage workers—they are central, not incidental, to the mission of your church.

Emotional Importance

Work gets emotional. It is a source of profound joy and heartbreak, accomplishment and stress, frustration and longing. At the end of a long day, we all know intuitively that our identity and emotions are deeply tied up in our daily work.

When workers enter the sanctuary, they carry a whole week of experiences and emotions—their projects and deadlines, their conflicts and confessions, their wins and losses. They will bear the weight of all this as they walk into your worship service. What happens next will depend largely on you.

Is your sanctuary a place where workers can talk with God about their workplace emotions? Can they bring their weekly triumphs and trials here? Do they know that these feelings are of any concern to God? Or must they pretend that their emotions do not exist?

They might do their level best to suppress their concerns. Through sheer force of will, they might try to be "extra spiritual" and forget about work for an hour. But, inevitably, their workplace heartaches, longings, and frustrations will bubble up. In their stories, we begin to sense *the emotional reason* why our worship should engage the questions of work.

Spiritual Importance

While our worship traditions vary, there is a universal Christian agreement that a central purpose of worship is something like "spiritual communion" with God. We long to walk and talk with our Lord as Adam and Eve did in the garden. As the psalmist says, "It is good to be near God" (Ps. 73:28). Worship, in other words, is a time of connection and conversation.

Now, consider for just a moment how normal human beings connect and begin a conversation. What are the questions they normally ask one another? *How was work this week? How are the markets looking? What's going on at the hospital? Business good?*

We do this for good reason. Work is incredibly important to us, and talking about it is a great way to build a meaningful connection with someone else. And this is exactly our point: If talking about work is how humans connect and commune with one another, it stands to reason that a central way they will connect and commune with God is by having an honest conversation with him about their daily work. The connection here is simple, but it's all too often missed. Every pastor wants their people to have deeper conversations with God in worship, and work is one of the best strategies for kickstarting that conversation. This is *the spiritual reason* your worship should engage workers.

Ethical Importance

Throughout their working lives, Christians encounter ethical questions and temptations. When faced with these complex issues, people often feel confused, fearful, and alone, and if isolated from Christian community and conversation, they begin to go their own way. They begin to imagine that God's commands apply in the sanctuary but not the workplace. Their career belongs to them, not God.

In ancient Israel, worship and ethics were meant to be one. Worship was supposed to be a training ground, a place where Israelites not only praised the Lord but learned to walk in his ways. The same is supposed to be true for Christian worship. In communion, we learn how to share and take turns. In the offering, we learn to live generously. In confession, we learn to say, "I was wrong . . . I hurt you . . . I'm sorry . . . I want to change." In the sermon, we learn how to listen to a story outside of our own. Bowing in prayer, we learn the posture of humility. Opening our hands, we learn the posture of dependence. We are not simply encouraged or fed in worship; in God's presence, *we are changed*.

While worship is supposed to transform and train us for ethical lives in the world, many worshipers simply don't experience it that way. They do not recognize that participation in worship commits us to an ethical way of walking through the world. One cannot experience the gracious hospitality of the Lord's Table and then go out on Monday to "get yours" at the corporate table. This is *the ethical reason* our worship must address the working lives of people. We cannot praise the gracious and generous work of Christ on Sunday and fail to reflect that work on Monday.

Pastoral Importance

There's actually a "selfish" reason pastors might want to lead worship for workers—it could make their own role more lighthearted.

We're constantly meeting pastors who are utterly exhausted and overworked. They are running countless programs, organizing committees, hosting church events, and rallying the troops week after week. They feel as if they're on an endless tour of recruiting people to get more involved inside the church. Success is defined by the amount of people and things they manage to bring into the church building. Recruitment mode can be profoundly exhausting because—quite frankly—it's never enough. These weary church leaders might look at a book like ours with some suspicion. "This book is going to add one more thing to my already full plate."

But that's not what we're doing. Rather than coaxing pastors and worship leaders to recruit more and more, this book calls them into the labor of blessing and sending.

As a leader in the church, your task is a humble one: to bless, equip, and send the servants of God. The flock you shepherd is already doing God's work. They are the holy priesthood. Christ's commission is on them, not just you. *You are not responsible for the mission of God in the community—they are.*

This book is not intended to increase your load. We want to help you shake off some of the unnecessary burden of being the endless recruiter, the only one in the church who works for God. Our hope is that this book will help you take on an easier yoke, the joy of blessing and sending God's people into the Lord's work. This is *the pastoral reason* for leading worship for workers.

Who Counts as a "Worker" in This Book?

But what about children, students, volunteers, stay-at-home parents, and the retired? Do they count as workers? Unequivocally yes. Our definition of a worker includes a wide range of callings and vocations. Some of these will be paid and some will not. All these roles, however, will include an exertion of effort, an improvement of skill, and a sense of responsibility for one's neighbor and the created world. Whether you are changing diapers, studying algebra, washing dishes, painting a landscape, volunteering in a soup kitchen, or caring for grandchildren, your labor can be a worthy offering of worship to the Lord. In this sense, *we all labor.*

We use the language of "work" and "workers" to highlight an extremely important aspect of the Christian life that has been almost entirely ignored in books about worship. But this discussion is not meant to exclude anyone. Quite the opposite. It is meant to recruit and remind children, stay-at-home parents, and the retired that while the economy of the world might not recognize or pay them for their labors, the economy of God most certainly sees and delights in their daily callings.

Regardless of pay, we all have gardens to care for, discoveries to make, wounds to bandage, monsters to fight, problems to solve, and chaos to put in order. Our diverse callings and tasks are sacred. God sees and delights in all our labors. We love God with our hearts, to be sure, but we also love him with our strength.

In this book and on our website, you will find worship resources that honor the sacred callings of children, students, volunteers, stay-at-home parents, and the retired. Regardless of pay, their labor is precious in the sight of God.

The Structure of the Book

This is a guide for action. It offers you the resources, ideas, and practices you will need to lead effective worship for workers. It's organized into five sections.

The first section, titled "Where Do We Start?" invites readers to begin by carefully examining their own congregations and contexts. Here we take an audit of your current worship practices: what is already going well and where you might have some opportunities to grow. This section also invites leaders to take a closer interest in the working lives of their people and the unique stories they are bringing with them into worship. Once you know what you are working with, you will be in a better position to understand which steps will move you forward.

The second section is the heart and soul of the book. Here we invite worship leaders and pastors to experience worship from an entirely different perspective—from that of the worker. You will follow congregants as they move through a worship service from the welcome to the dismissal. In this section, we offer a wide range of ideas for how your times of welcome and praise, confession and prayer, offering and communion, blessing and benediction can all engage workers more deeply. Even if all these elements are not present in your particular context each week, our hope is that these chapters will help deepen your current practices in new and creative ways.

The third section explores how you might bless and commission specific callings and careers in your congregation. Perhaps the school year is about to begin and you want to bless all of your teachers. Perhaps it's tax time and you want to bless your accountants. Perhaps your congregation has a lot of factory workers, medical professionals, or software engineers in need of attention and prayer. This section will give you the tools you need to set aside some special time in worship to bless and pray for them.

The fourth section is titled "Creative Ideas for Deeper Engagement," and it is precisely that. While many of our suggestions are subtle and safe, these ideas are a bit more demanding. In these chapters, you will find a wide range of creative (and sometimes disruptive) ideas to challenge a congregation's assumptions about the divisions between faith and work, sacred and secular.

We close with a brief guide for group discussion. The task of deepening a congregation's work and worship is a big one. It should not be done alone. Solitary individuals working to "change worship" are nearly guaranteed to fail. So, grab a crew of elders, pastors, workers, and musicians and discuss this book *together*.

How to Read (and Not to Read) This Book

There are several different approaches for how you might engage with the material in this book.

1. You can hop around from chapter to chapter depending on what you need for a particular Sunday. Perhaps you are preparing for Sunday morning and you need a prayer of blessing for your high school graduates, your veterans, or your medical professionals—we have a chapter that can help you with that. Perhaps you are in search of a creative way to honor all the retirees and their service to the community in worship—we've got it. As you read, feel welcome to jump directly to chapters that interest you and meet your immediate needs. That said, while we give you permission to hunt and peck, we want to offer you two other options for a deeper and more transformative approach to the book.

2. You can choose to read this book slowly from cover to cover. As you journey through its pages, you can begin to learn more about the *why*, even as you practice the *how*, of leading worship for workers. Readers who choose this path will be equipped to do much more than simply find and insert a good resource about our daily callings. If you read slowly, you will be equipped to write your own prayers and blessings about work. Through you and your creativity, your people will receive prayers and liturgies that are uniquely crafted just for them.

3. While the first two methods are great, our deepest hope is that you might find some companions in your church to read and discuss this book with you. After all, if only one member of a church is passionate about reconnecting worship and work, the prospects of real and lasting change are low. Worship design, properly understood, is a team sport. Deep and transformational worship requires communal participation and creativity. Consider inviting a musician to join your reading group, someone from a pastoral care team, a missions committee leader, and someone from the college or women's ministry. This isn't limited to worship leaders only. A diversity of voices of people working inside and outside the church building will only strengthen your engagement with this book. So, go find some friends who are up for an adventure.

While there are a wide variety of ways to engage this book, we are concerned that it might be misread in ways that could be destructive. With that in mind, here are a few brief words of warning.

1. **Don't read this book as a critique of your current worship practices.** We don't want you to feel guilty or defensive as you read our work. Instead, we want you to feel invited into a wide range of ways that you can deepen and enrich your current practices of worship. Don't be overly critical of yourself or your congregation; rather, view this as an opportunity to enrich and deepen the many great things you are already doing.

2. **Don't read this book as a massive to-do list.** These diverse ideas and resources should be exciting, not exhausting. You don't have to do everything in this book. In fact, you shouldn't. Some of these ideas will never work in your church—and that is perfectly okay. When you come across a worship resource that doesn't fit, either toss it out or consider it a creative opportunity to imagine what might actually work in your congregation.

3. **Don't read this book as a panacea.** This book is not a cure-all for every problem in work and in worship. Be realistic about what a single Sunday morning can actually accomplish. This book talks a lot about the power of worship—the many things it can and should accomplish in God's people. Yet, while worship is indeed powerful, readers have to acknowledge the finite impact of a single Sunday morning. Ultimately, workers will be transformed by Christ alone. Worship for workers is not the answer—Jesus is. Which leads to our final warning.

4. **Don't read this book as a distraction from the primary purpose of worship.** Christ alone is the beginning and end of Christian worship. Our worship should be directed only to him. We have no interest whatsoever in making worship "about work and workers." We have no interest in taking attention away from God. This book is specifically designed to help workers direct the entirety of their lives and labor to the mission and glory of Christ, where all things ultimately belong.

Of course, there will be some who claim that, if Christian worship is to remain holy and pure, it must remain completely detached from and disinterested in work and the things of earth. To these critics our reply is rather simple. Ignoring our work lives will not make your worship holy or pure. Instead, it will allow your congregants to live under a dangerous misconception: "While my Sunday worship belongs to God, my Monday work belongs to me." *Our book does not distract from Christ; it redirects the whole of our lives to him.*

Finally, remember that this is a handbook. You can and should write in it. Make sure you have a sturdy pen and a curious mind at the ready. We will provide you with ample space for reflection and ideation throughout the book. Before we jump in, write down what stood out to you in this first chapter. If you have got questions or concerns, note them here. If the ideas are already coming, write them down before they're gone.

_____

_____

_____

_____

_____

_____

_____

_____

_____

2

Auditing Your Worship

Worship leaders have the best (and the worst) seat in the house. From the front of the sanctuary we can see everyone's face. We see faces that are fully alive and fully engaged in worship. We see faces that are tired and worn out from an exhausting week. We see the faces of those who weep, who are barely able to hold it together. We see frosty spouses who are putting on a good face. These are our people, and, for an hour or two each week, we truly see them. It lifts our spirits, but it also breaks our hearts.

As we sit down to plan yet another worship service or write another sermon, these faces excite us and haunt us. We plan worship with and for real people with real lives in a real community.

Good worship leadership requires that we know what is going on behind these faces and, on a broader scale, within our cities. Good worship planning demands a level of care and creativity to craft prayers and worship elements that speak to *these* people's lives and worlds.

Before we can lead worship that truly engages people, we need to begin with an honest assessment of who and what we are working with. We need to audit our worship and our workers. Are our current worship practices connecting with workers and impacting their daily lives? Moreover, who are our worshipers? Where do they work? What are their struggles and questions, their loves and longings? What are they bringing with them into the sanctuary?

If you're worried that this audit will make you feel bad about your current worship leadership, don't be. *This audit is not meant to bring a sense of shame or diminish the good work that you are already doing.* It is simply meant to help you reflect honestly about where your community is so that you can approach the rest of this handbook with a sense of purpose and direction. Worship planning is a journey, not a destination. As pastors and worship leaders, we never arrive. We're always growing, learning, and listening to the Spirit's nudgings.

This chapter will help you take a careful accounting of the (dis)connections between your worship practices and the everyday lives of your people. Here we will help you identify your unique strengths and weaknesses, opportunities and threats in this specific area. The next chapter will turn our attention to the diverse callings and careers in your congregation. What do your congregants do all day? What challenges are they facing? What questions and burdens are they bringing into worship? What testimonies of grace and transformation might they share with your church?

Identifying Your Strengths

When focusing on deepening a community's worship, we should always start from a position of encouragement on what that community does well rather than judgment of its liturgical failures. As we work to deepen our worship, we will need some strong starting points, some footholds, if you will.

In the space below, reflect on two or three things your congregation does really *well* in worship. What are your liturgical high points? What are the unique moments in worship where you can tell that your people are fully engaged? This exercise is important. We're not simply trying to make you feel good about yourself. We want you to identify what your people know how to do really well in worship. They might be great at sharing their testimony. Maybe you have people who love to sing. Perhaps you are highly intergenerational and enjoy broad participation of all ages. Or perhaps the Lord's Supper is a particularly loved and powerful time for your people. Name these strengths. These will be your building blocks for further growth.

Name two or three elements of worship that are deeply meaningful to your people, explaining why you think these moments are particularly resonant.

1. _____

_____

_____

2. _____
_____
_____

3. _____
_____
_____

Now, write about one or two specific ways that your worship services already speak to the lived experience of your people in the world. At what point in the worship service do you mention the world outside and the concerns of everyday life? Be as specific as you can.

1. _____
_____
_____
_____
_____

2. _____
_____
_____
_____
_____

Identifying Your Weaknesses

Now comes the uncomfortable part. What are the *weaknesses* in your worship service? When do people seem most disengaged? How has your worship become detached from the lived experience and daily realities of your people and your community? How are you perpetuating the divide between Sunday and Monday, between worship and work?

Now, we obviously don't know anything about your church. It would be presumptuous of us to tell you exactly how your worship might be falling short of connecting with your people. That said, there are common mistakes that we regularly witness in churches. Take some time to read through these brief statements and consider which ring true for you and which ring true for your congregation. Remember, these categories are not comprehensive or mutually exclusive, so several may resonate to some degree or another.

Institutional worship. These worship services overemphasize the work of the gathered church, the institution. These services are always recruiting people to get more involved in the programs going on inside the church building. They ignore the daily work of the scattered church laboring outside in the community. The "real" work of God is done by the institution and the church staff—its elders, deacons, missionaries, worship leaders, and the like. God transforms people inside the church, not outside it. So join our programs! The message of worship is subtle but clear: Your work will have meaning when you work inside the institution alongside church staff. Both conservative and progressive churches are guilty of this. Conservatives elevate the work of missionaries, progressives the work of activists. Regardless of ideology, the diverse callings and careers of the people scattered throughout the city are forgotten.

Spiritualized worship. Spiritual things matter. Material things do not. The sanctuary is a sacred and spiritual place. The outside world is sinful and secular. Sunday morning is a time of spiritual escape from a material world that is passing away. When workers enter the sanctuary, they should check all their material concerns at the door. It is time to be spiritual. As the old hymn says, "This world is not my home, I'm just passing through."

Saccharine worship. Worship must always be happy and exciting. Worship is a thing of joy and celebration. There's no lament or crying allowed—no space for silence. Saccharine worship paints a sweet, rosy, and *dishonest* picture of the Christian life. Worshipers must suppress the painful reality of their daily lives and labor. They must put on a brave face and speak to God with nothing but joy and gratitude. Be happy, no questions or crying allowed.

Passive worship. Worship is a spectator sport—a matter of entertainment rather than engagement. Instead of being invited into a dialogue with God, workers are encouraged to sit back and passively consume a "worship experience." Pastors and musicians perform excellent sermons and songs on behalf of their people. Congregants have nothing to do but sit back, relax, and enjoy the show. Involving them in worship would muck up the excellent performance.

Private worship. Worship is a private act of personal devotion. Private worship ignores the public consequences of what we say and do in the sanctuary. A worker can happily sing songs and pray prayers of tremendous grace and hospitality and never see that they have an obligation to share that grace or hospitality with their coworkers the next day. Private worship also ignores the public realities of the world outside the walls of the sanctuary. Your local economy might be in free fall and thousands might be laid off, but inside the walls of private worship one would never know. Private worship never mentions the public challenges workers are facing outside the church. It is a place where we pretend the public does not exist.

Intellectual worship. The focus here is on teaching and education. Sermons are focused on ideas and theology; they tend to be didactic and often quite long. Success is defined by the amount of theological information implanted into the brains of the people. Good worship is the effective transfer of a biblical worldview from the pastor to the people. Equipped with the correct theological ideas, people are able to think biblically in the world. Their emotions, their stories and imagination, their hearts' deep sense of guilt, heartbreak, and longing—these things are left untouched. Intellectual worship can theologically educate a worker's mind, but it cannot shape their heart and life.

Obviously, these six types don't reflect reality. These are cartoon churches. No congregation fits these types perfectly (thanks be to God). Real congregations are far more complex. We share these six categories simply to help illuminate potential weaknesses in your worship. We also hope it is plain to see that every worship style can fail. Every denomination can stumble. When it comes to detaching worship from everyday life, there are a variety of ways to fall short.

Once again, this list is not intended to guilt or shame anyone. We're not looking to point fingers. Nor are we giving you ammunition for an unfriendly congregational fight over worship—we've had more than enough of those. No, we offer up these diverse shortcomings to illuminate the complex challenges that lie before all of us. This is a messy process, and sometimes it helps to just disentangle and name the issues with clarity.

1. Having read through each of these, which ones most accurately reflect your congregation's struggle to integrate worship and work? Include specific contextual details as to why this might be.

_____

_____

_____

_____

_____

2. Now reflect for a moment on your own struggle to connect work and worship. Are you personally drawn into or tempted by one or two of these forms of worship? How might you be contributing to this issue?

_____

_____

_____

_____

_____

Discovering Your Opportunities

Now that you've identified some of the reasons why your worship has been disengaged from the lives and labor of those outside the sanctuary, it's time to think about where you might want to go and (more importantly) how to actually get there.

Below is a simple chart that identifies shifts *away* from the problems you just identified *toward* healthier patterns for engaging workers in worship.

Institutional   ⟶   Scattered

Spiritual   ⟶   Material

Saccharine   ⟶   Honest

Passive   ⟶   Participatory

Private   ⟶   Public

Intellectual   ⟶   Holistic

If your worship has an institutional bent, you have an opportunity to imagine new ways to highlight, celebrate, and bless the important work of the scattered church in the community.

If your worship has had a spiritual emphasis, you have an opportunity to imagine new ways to welcome and engage with the raw stuff and mundane materiality of daily work during worship.

If your worship is typically saccharine, you have an opportunity to imagine new ways to honestly name the thorns and thistles of work in the world, to create spaces on Sunday morning for real tears and longing.

If your worship is more on the passive side, you have an opportunity to imagine new ways to create a sense of widespread ownership, agency, and participation in your congregational worship.

If your worship has had a private focus, you have an opportunity to imagine new ways you can acknowledge the challenges of life in your community and the public consequences of your songs, prayers, and vows in the sanctuary.

If your worship is ordinarily intellectual, you have an opportunity to imagine new ways in which your worship can move beyond the brain to the whole person—their hearts and souls, bodies and bones.

Of course, it is one thing to identify the need for a bridge between worship and the individual, and it is another thing entirely to actually build it. That is what this book is all about—giving you the tools, resources, and ideas you need to construct these bridges.

While this book will provide you with many new ideas and resources for deepening your worship, we first want to encourage you to start from your own assets and strengths. Allowing these opportunities to emerge from their own native soil is the best way to develop a strong root system for thriving worship. The first step in this journey, your primary opportunity for growth, will come from something both you and your congregation already do well, something you know and are comfortable with. Start with what you love and go from there. This is the place of opportunity.

Name two or three "from/to" goals for yourself and your congregation.

1. _____

   _____

2. _____

   _____

3. _____

   _____

Recognizing the Threats to Worship

Deepening a community's worshiping life is never easy. Every pastor and worship leader will face barriers and obstacles when implementing changes. We should never be surprised when we face these challenges. It's part of the gig. As you endeavor to deepen your community's worship, what threats might you face? Resistance might very well come from multiple directions. Here we encourage you to audit your potential threats at four distinct levels:

1. Name some of the ways the broader culture of your country or local community might resist the deep integration of worship and work.

   a. _____

   _____

   b. _____

   _____

   c. _____

   _____

2. Name some of the ways the people in your church might struggle to understand or appreciate this connection between worship and work.

   a. _____

   _____

   b. _____

   _____

   c. _____

   _____

3. Name some of the ways your church leadership might struggle to understand or appreciate this connection between worship and work.

   a. _____

   _____

   b. _____

   _____

   c. _____

   _____

4. Name some of the ways you personally might threaten the deep integration of worship and work in your community. What are some ways you might hold yourself back from leading this process well?

   a. _____

   _____

b. _____

_____

c. _____

_____

Having conducted a careful audit of your community's worshiping life, we can now turn our attention to learning more about the diverse callings and careers in your community.

3

Auditing Your Workers

As you lead worship, you look out over a sea of faces. But do you know what these faces have seen and experienced this past week? Do you know what they are anticipating next week? Do you know their diverse careers and callings? Their giftings and passions? The ways they uniquely contribute to the life of your community?

We can't answer these questions without a deeper examination of our people. After all, how can our worship provide a word of encouragement or comfort when we don't know the burdens they're carrying?

As an exercise, grab a printed list of your church members. Work your way through the various names and faces. Do you know what these people do for work? What do they study? Where do they serve? Sketch out as many careers and callings as you can. Remember that students, stay-at-home parents, the retired, and the unemployed all count as "workers." We all have callings, even if we are not paid. We've provided some basic categories to keep you organized. If these categories don't fit your people, by all means, create your own!

Healing	Learning	Building
Selling	Protecting	Managing
Fixing	Creating	Other_____
Hosting	Serving	Other_____

As you look over the lists you've created, reflect on what these workers might carry with them into worship on Sundays. Under each category, name some of the potential joys and challenges of their professions. Take a guess (even if it's uneducated). Think about their primary sources of excitement and stress.

Healing	Learning	Building
Selling	Protecting	Managing
Fixing	Creating	Other_____
Hosting	Serving	Other_____

Finally, think for a moment about what these workers might say to God about their work, then consider what God might say back to them. Sketch out a few phrases for each category.

Healing	Learning	Building
Selling	Protecting	Managing
Fixing	Creating	Other_____
Hosting	Serving	Other_____

Now take a step outside your sanctuary doors and consider the city or neighborhood around the church. Maybe even take a walk or a quick drive around your community. Imagine your congregants as workers and consumers in these spaces.

1. List the most prominent industries you see in your community (agricultural, industrial, medical, service, academic, etc.).

   _____

   _____

   _____

   _____

   _____

2. What are some of the virtues and vices of your most prominent industries?

   _____

   _____

   _____

   _____

   _____

3. Is there a seasonal rhythm to any of these industries? Is there a high and low season? A period of stress? A time of plenty?

   _____

   _____

   _____

   _____

   _____

4. What sorts of spiritual and theological questions do these industries pose to Christians who engage them?

   _____

   _____

   _____

   _____

How are you feeling after completing this section? Are you overwhelmed or excited? A little of both? Either way, knowing your people is important work. This handbook will continue to call you back to having a greater understanding of the working lives of your people as you lead worship that speaks to their daily callings.

Remember, this is slow and patient work. A radical shift in worship style and language is never wise. It will be jarring and confusing for the congregation. Spiritual formation does not happen overnight. The Lord will slowly form them (and you!) over time. Read carefully and compassionately over your congregation's strengths and weaknesses, build on what you do well, pick some footholds, and find some "low-hanging fruit." Start there. There's good work to be done. Let's begin!

An Audit for the Eager

If you are eager for a more in-depth audit of workers in your congregation, you might consider the following resource. Made to Flourish is a nationwide network of churches that care deeply about workers and their place within the mission of God. Over the years they have developed an innovative online survey called Scatter that is useful for auditing an entire congregation.

Through this online survey tool, you can collect and visualize the full breadth of your congregation's diverse gifts, callings, and careers. Whether your church is large or small, rural or urban, engaging with this survey can provide a profound benefit. This assessment allows you to quickly identify what each member does throughout the week and the unique gifts, passions, and hidden talents they bring to the people of God. After taking the survey, one congregant reported, "This is the only church survey I've ever taken that I actually enjoyed."

An Audit for the Creative

If you are more creatively inclined, you can develop a "vocational word cloud" for your congregation. There are multiple free websites where you can input a list of callings and careers in your congregation, and they will generate a beautiful word cloud for you. Mentimeter is a website that will let your congregation create a word cloud in real time *during worship* through a scanned

QR code. You could go further and make a separate word cloud for vocational joys and one for vocational sorrows that each person carries into worship with them. Project the word clouds on the screen and use them to help you pray for your congregation that Sunday.

Administrative Staff
Rancher Cowboys **Web Developer** Truancy Coordinator
Director of Integration Government Worker Occupational Therapist
Scientist Realtor Contractor **Financial Advisor** Software Architect
Principal **Professor** Pastor **Nurse** Unsure Intern **Truck Driver** Electrician
Plumber Therapist Homeless **Student** **Retired** Musician Retail Salesperson Physician Medical
Lawyer **Teacher** **Farmer** Surgeon
Fire Marshall Journalist
Healthcare **Business Owner** **IT Support** Stay at Home Parent
Sailor Engineer **Doctor** CFO Bartender Social Worker Mother Builder
Dancer Police Consultant Architect High School Teacher Counselor
Special Ed Teacher Digital Media Coordinator
Custodian

Figure 3.1. Sample word cloud

PART 2

WORKERS MOVE THROUGH WORSHIP

4

Workers Gather

First Words Matter

> Good morning, everyone. Welcome to worship. We know you have had a long
> week of parenting, working, and serving. We know you have a lot of projects,
> deadlines, errands, and responsibilities on your minds and hearts. But for the
> next hour, we invite you to leave that at the door and focus on God.

While it's rarely explicit, workers often believe that sanctuaries have a rather
strict dress code. They show up, doing their best to disrobe. Entering the
sanctuary, they try hard not to think about work, deadlines, and stressors from
the week. The beauty and brokenness of their offices, hospitals, classrooms,
and factory floors need to be left at the door. Workday life is not welcome
here. They need to take off their uniform and put on something more pious.
Not surprisingly, the clothes rarely feel like their own.

How should we welcome these workers into worship? How do we tell them
not to leave their work at the door? How do we encourage them to honestly
carry it before the Lord in worship?

The first few sentences of a service are critical. They frame the entire purpose of worship and its connection to our lives in the world. The opening
words communicate what we think about God, about ourselves, and about
our purpose for being gathered together in worship. Too often these are throw-
away words of welcome, uttered by whomever is first up to the microphone

and tasked with getting the service started. Mindfulness and preparation can turn these words into a rich invitation to worship that not only falls fresh on Sunday morning but also prepares workers to recognize God's presence and power on Monday.

A great welcome will connect the week we all just experienced with our God and our worship in a meaningful way. This is the task of the welcome: to form a critically important bridge between our week, our worship, and our God.

- **Our Week**
  Young and old, rich and poor, we are all carrying our week with us into the sanctuary. We do not need to hide from that reality or pretend as though it does not exist. Good welcomes will invite honest reflection on the past week and real truth telling about its highs and lows—the burdens that weigh us down and the triumphs for which we raise our hands in praise. Nothing needs to be "left at the door." Crossing the threshold of the sanctuary is not an escape from the world. You are not entering a space where the things of earth grow strangely dim. Rather, this welcome to worship positively invites God's people to honestly carry their week of work, service, and study before the Lord in all its beauty, ugliness, and everything in between.

- **Our Worship**
  An impactful welcome will invite people to wholeheartedly carry their ordinary labor before the Lord. They don't need to disrobe and enter worship in ill-fitting, pious clothes. They can (indeed, they *must!*) carry their working lives to the altar. This is a place where they can bring workplace triumphs, breakthroughs, and joys. It is also a place where they can humbly bring workplace confessions, heartbreaks, and laments. God not only allows workers to approach—he beckons them and rejoices over their presence. The sanctuary is the place where God speaks to them, feeds them, and sends them out with blessing and purpose. Worship is for workers.

- **Our God**
  God has been present and active with his people all week long. God has not been waiting patiently in the sanctuary for his people to return. Nor is God waiting in heaven for his people to call or welcome him into the

Words of Gathering

The Lord be with you.
And also with you.
God has gathered us here today,
a day in which we bring our full selves—
our simplicity, our complexity,
our joy, our sadness,
our vigilance, our apathy,
our hopes, our fears.
In the midst of our own stories,
we gather here to be found in God's story—
a God who welcomes all people,
a God who loves all people without conditions, and beyond
   measure.
So let us gather, and let us worship.
Amen.

Nelson Robert Cowan, *Worship Any Time Any Place*
(Abingdon Press, 2024), 32. Used with permission.

Worker Welcome

Children of God,
Bring it to the altar and come as you are.
Bring your whole selves, your whole week—your sorrows and
      your joys.

Don't hide that which preoccupies you,
don't ignore that which burdens.

Bring your whole self to the altar:
   your work and your responsibilities,
   your victories and your triumphs.

God desires that you enter here with fullness of heart.
Bring your stories of salvation and sadness.
Come and give them to the Lord.

sanctuary. It is God who has called them back into the sanctuary. He was with them in their work and he is now with them in their worship. God is the ever-present and faithful initiator of this relationship, not the other way around. When workers leave the sanctuary, God continues to go before, beside, and behind them, inviting them to worship through their daily work. It is not our duty to convince God to show up in our work or our worship. It's our privilege to be invited by the One who has been—and continues to be—present by his grace. God invites; we respond.

This is not nearly as difficult as it might sound. Consider the welcome that appears at the beginning of this chapter and how a very simple edit would completely transform its impact.

Good morning, everyone. Welcome to worship. We know you have had a long week of parenting, working, and serving. We know you have a lot of projects, deadlines, errands, and responsibilities on your minds and hearts. For the next hour, we invite you *to carry your week before the Lord in worship.*

Consider the following words of greeting that simply and clearly communicate these three truths:

Example 1: Our gracious God has been present with you in your daily living throughout the whole of your week. You have never been alone. So whether you come exhausted or full, anxious or at peace, God's gracious invitation to come and worship calls you to bring it all before the Lord.

Example 2: As God gathers us for worship, I invite you to a few moments of silence as you reflect on your last week of work, of parenting, of daily living. [Silence] The God who has been present with you through the whole of your week welcomes you to worship. Here you lay before him your burdens and your triumphs, that you might once again know the abiding presence of our gracious God.

Your first words are of primary importance, preparing the worker's heart for worship. In the space below, take some time to practice.

Try a Few of Your Own "Rewrites"

Sample: Thanks for coming, everyone. It's time to worship.

Rewrite: _____
_____

Sample: Good morning, everyone. It's been a long week, and we need this time to just focus on God. Let's worship.

Rewrite: _____
_____

Sample: Hello, church. Let's join our voices loud enough for God and all the world to hear. We need to worship, and we need to do it now.

Rewrite: _____
_____

Reframing Exercise

Many churches begin their worship services with Scripture. The Bible has an abundance of invitations to God's people to enter, worship, and praise. Psalm 100 is a wonderful example of a scriptural call to worship. It reminds us of God's goodness and faithfulness, which ground our worship and exhort us to praise. Consider ways you might frame this classic psalm of praise, and eventually others, to speak to the reality of the worker's daily life.

[**Name several vocations . . . students, carpenters, etc.**]
Shout for joy to the LORD, all the earth.
[**Name several more vocations . . .**]
Worship the LORD with gladness;
come before him with joyful songs.
Know that the LORD is God.
It is he who made us, and we are his;
we are his people, the sheep of his pasture.
[**We are his** _____ **(vocation), the** _____ **of his** _____.]

Enter his gates with thanksgiving
[**Enter his gates with** _____ (**work artifact**)]
   and his courts with praise;
   give thanks to him and praise his name.
For the LORD is good and his love endures forever;
[**From the moment you** _____ **to the time you** _____]
   his faithfulness continues through all generations.

Write down one or two of your frequently used calls to worship or opening words.

1. _____

   _____

   _____

2. _____

   _____

   _____

What are they missing and how can you make them more impactful for workers? Edit/rewrite below.

1. _____

   _____

   _____

2. _____

   _____

   _____

Get Creative

How a worker travels to worship can deeply affect how they engage with God. Have you ever paused to consider how your congregation shows up for worship on a Sunday morning? Are they hurried and distracted? Have they even considered the significance of what they are about to do? A few minutes of mindful preparation can ready their hearts to receive God's gracious invitation to worship. Script an invitation to worship that you could project on your screens as people walk into the sanctuary.

5

Workers Sing

My hymnal doesn't have a song for federal contractors.

I (Katie) served as a worship pastor for twenty years in Washington, DC. Not surprisingly, our church was filled with federal employees who worked at various levels of national government. On my very first Labor Day Sunday, I wanted to design a special worship service that focused on the "work of the people." I was disappointed—but not at all surprised—that there were no songs highlighting the good and important work of government services. After all, who doesn't appreciate well-functioning transportation systems, food safety regulations, and Yellowstone National Park? The same was true for a friend leading worship in Seattle. There aren't any great hymns about software development or a well-crafted latte. Perhaps it's a rhyming issue.

The more I dug, the more I realized that the only church songs related to work refer almost entirely to the life of a farmer. These songs speak of working in the fields of the Lord, planting seeds, tilling soil, and bringing in God's harvest. While this is great for churches in agricultural communities, it does nothing for those in more urban contexts. Accountants and health care administrators have to use their creativity to imagine what sowing and reaping look like in their particular fields. When it comes to songs about spreadsheets and cost projections, the worship song selection is slim pickings.

Why is this? Why does the church have an abundance of agricultural songs and nothing for our work in parenting, truck driving, and middle management? The answer is quite simple: The church stopped writing work songs about a hundred years ago.

The church used to be fluent in congregational work songs. Medieval Europe had many of them. The African American church was quite literally born singing work songs in the fields amid the terror of slavery. One can find rich collections of work songs in Latin American, Asian, and African churches. Even ancient Israel had its share of work songs; the psalms are filled with references to farming, shepherding, irrigating, trading, and building. But modern churches throughout the West abruptly stopped writing work songs, emptying our repertoires of vocational songs with Monday in mind.

Whole books have been written analyzing the trends of congregational singing in the last century. There has been a marked shift in both content and style that has deeply affected worshipers on many levels. Increasingly passive, we sing less and listen to others more. We sing as individuals, not as communities. We sing our gratitude but tend to bury our laments. This has had a variety of consequences, one being the devastating (and growing) divide between the sacred and the secular, the spiritual and the material, Sunday and Monday.

Worship for Workers, the organization we have founded, is trying hard to right this wrong, one song at a time. We have collaborated with a creative collective of songwriters called The Porter's Gate. Together, we've produced a beautiful portfolio of new work songs for the church. We have hosted songwriting retreats with creatives and launched a search contest specifically focused on "sending songs." They all live on our website free for download and use in your context. Our deep hope is that this library not only grows but also inspires more songwriters to take seriously the call to reintegrate the language of work into the church's songs.

While we hope these new songs will be an encouragement to worship leaders everywhere, the problem still remains. Sunday is coming quickly and you need to pick three songs. You can only work with the songs you have, not the songs you want. So what do you do in the meantime? How do you make do with what you have?

A Balanced Diet of Song

Worship scholar John Witvliet often says that, on average, a congregation has a rotation of about two hundred songs in its "song diet."[1] These are the songs they know and can sing well. That might seem like a large number, but when you remove all the Christmas carols, Easter hymns, and season-specific songs, that number diminishes rapidly. As a result, you should be very picky about what songs you choose to include in your church's very limited song diet. What we sing in worship shapes and forms us over time. The lyrics and melodies resonate in our souls long after we depart the building.

In the space below, list the songs sung most often in your congregation.

1. _____
2. _____
3. _____
4. _____
5. _____
6. _____
7. _____
8. _____
9. _____
10. _____

As you look over your list, ponder the following questions.

- Which of these songs will help workers recognize and name the goodness of God in their work?
- Which of these songs help workers name their heartbreaks, confessions, and laments?
- Which ones help workers articulate and live out the redemption of God in their workplace?
- Which songs do you want on your people's lips as they wake up for work and school on Monday?

1. John Witvliet, "The Nuts and Bolts of Worship Planning," Calvin Institute of Christian Worship, February 10, 2001, https://worship.calvin.edu/resources/articles/nuts-and-bolts-worship-planning.

- Which songs will sustain and guide them best through a long week of work?
- Is your top ten, and broader song diet, balanced enough to give workers what they need to express the full range of their emotions and experiences to God? What is missing from your list?

Song Framing

In all likelihood, none of your top ten songs mention work or vocation. With that limitation in mind, how might you take your existing songs and deepen their vocational impact?

Enter the practice of song framing.

A song "frame" is a device used by worship leaders to provide a short verbal introduction or conclusion to a particular congregational song. When used well, a good framing can enable a congregation of singers to approach a familiar song in an unfamiliar way. A few well-chosen words at the outset can transform how the worshiper enters the song and the sorts of things they carry with them into its melodic world.

For example, let's look at a classic hymn, "Take My Life and Let It Be." Imagine that you invited your congregation to take a few moments to think about one task, one person, or one goal in their life and work that is particularly meaningful and important to them. Something they hold to rather tightly, perhaps *too* tightly. Invite them to carry that item into this song and ask God to take it and let it be consecrated and made holy for him. How might this new and unfamiliar framing transform a very familiar song?

As a worship leader, you have the creative ability to introduce and reframe these familiar songs in new and creative ways. In doing so, you are prompting your people to sing nonvocational songs through the lens of their daily living and work.

Since many worship services begin with a more upbeat selection of "praise and worship" songs, let's start there. As you invite workers into a time of praise, invite them to consider God's blessings and provisions from the past week. How has God made a way where there was none? Here they have an opportunity to pause and thank God—not themselves—for these breakthroughs. Invite them to consider a very tangible blessing that they have received in and from their work. With that blessing in hand, invite them to celebrate, honor, and offer thanksgiving to God for the good work he has accomplished.

What might this actually sound like? Below we provide a few examples to get your creativity flowing. We've found it helpful to begin by determining the song's primary message and then craft a framing that is more vocationally conversant.

Song Title: "Great Are You Lord"
The Song's Message: The Spirit's breath in our lungs prompts us to pour out our praise.
Vocational Framing: The Spirit's breath has sustained us all week, and that same breath will go before us and with us toward whatever this next week might hold. With the Spirit's help, we pour out our praise to our faithful and worthy God both today and all week long.

Song Title: "Praise to the Lord, the Almighty"
The Song's Message: The almighty Lord who promises to "prosper your work and defend you" is already at work in all of creation.
Vocational Framing: The King of all is at work in this creation and in this very city. God is inviting us to participate. In our work, our schools, and our communities, we ponder anew what the Almighty is doing—and we rejoice. Let's join our voices together in song.

Using these examples, select three songs you listed above in your top ten and practice a few vocational framings of your own with some work-, community-, and world-oriented language.

Song Title:
The Song's Message: _____
_____

Vocational Framing: _____
_____
_____
_____
_____

Song Title:
The Song's Message: _____

_____

Vocational Framing: _____

_____

_____

_____

_____

Song Title:
The Song's Message: _____

_____

Vocational Framing: _____

_____

_____

_____

_____

Short Songs for Long Impact

It's quite possible that while you were answering the questions above, a line of a song came to mind. Maybe a refrain stood out or a particular verse from a beloved hymn. There is no rule that says you have to sing an entire song from start to finish! Short song sections can have a long impact. Their abbreviated nature means they are easy to memorize and easy to remember. They can be learned and repeated on Sunday with the goal of becoming the spiritual soundtrack for Monday. Weave them into a prayer, a Scripture passage, or another liturgical element.

Here's an example of how you might close a worship service with a creative reappropriation of the song "In Christ Alone" by Keith Getty and Stuart Townend.[2] Here we take a familiar song, chop its last verse into pieces, and insert vocational framings directly into its heart:

2. Keith Getty and Stuart Townend, "In Christ Alone," © 2002 Thankyou Music Ltd. All rights reserved. Used with permission.

Leader Speaks: As we prepare to be sent out from this place to wherever God is calling us this week, we can go with confidence. For we know that we go with the power of Christ within us, and with the presence of God, through the Spirit who holds our destiny in the security of his hands.

People Sing: No guilt in life, no fear in death
This is the power of Christ in me
From life's first cry to final breath
Jesus commands my destiny.

Leader Speaks: In these moments of silence, I invite you to think through what your next week might hold at work, at school, at home. Pull out your calendar on your phone and glance through your week. Think about what you are looking forward to, what you are dreading, what you might be scared about. [Silence] In this coming week, in all our comings and our goings, may we call to mind this promise:

People Sing: No guilt in life, no fear in death
This is the power of Christ in me
From life's first cry to final breath
Jesus commands my destiny.

Leader Speaks: Go—confident of this, that he who began a good work in you will carry it on to completion until the day of Christ Jesus (Phil. 1:6). May the power and love of Christ go with you this day and forever. Amen.

People Sing: No guilt in life, no fear in death
This is the power of Christ in me
From life's first cry to final breath
Jesus commands my destiny.
No power of hell, no human plan
Can ever pluck me from His hand
Till He returns or calls me home
Here in the love of Christ I'll stand.

6

Workers Praise

While some workers enter the sanctuary feeling exhausted and frustrated, others will enter with a spirit of energy and accomplishment. They just got a promotion, made a big sale, signed a new contract, or had a breakthrough with one of their students. Some recently finished their degree, others are celebrating retirement, and still others successfully walked a child through the (seemingly endless) process of potty training. Whatever it is, workers will enter into worship carrying some sort of victory bubbling up within their souls.

After a major victory in ancient Israel, it was particularly important for the warriors to blow trumpets of praise. They would also set up celebratory piles of stones called "ebenezers." These rituals were a tangible and concrete way to mark and remember the Lord's victory. Beyond just a ritual, these memorials played a critically important function in the life of the people. The "stones of help" stood to remind God's people of the help they had received. This particular victory did not belong to them but to the Lord. It was *God* who rescued *them*. The trumpets of praise were sounded to audibly alert the people that God had indeed proved himself faithful once again. It was *God* who was worthy of praise.

"I got promoted!" "I graduated!" "I'm starting a new business!" So shouts social media. In ancient Israel, they reached for a trumpet; today we reach for our phones. While it can be self-centered, there can be something beautiful in the childlike excitement of a worker who has finally experienced a real breakthrough. Celebration and praise are a natural and wonderful part of human life and work. Whenever we experience success, it is absolutely inevitable that we will look for trumpets to blow. The real question is this: In which direction will the trumpet of praise be pointed? Will we praise and celebrate God or ourselves?

Imagine, if you will, a child encountering her first trumpet. She examines it carefully, presses the valve buttons, and inspects its various features. She thinks she is ready to play it, so she picks it up and lifts it to her lips. The first thing she must learn is how to hold it correctly. If she blows in the wrong end, she will get nothing but a face full of air. While there are many developmental stages to come for this novice trumpet player, none is more foundational than aiming her instrument in the correct direction.

Workplaces sometimes become spaces of toxic self-promotion and self-adulation. They can train workers to hold their trumpets backward. In such environments, workers are taught to proclaim their own accomplishments and ignore their utter dependence on the work of God and their coworkers. In the end, blowing the wrong way into the trumpet does no one any good.

Here is where Sunday morning can help.

First, Sunday morning can slowly train workers how to hold their trumpets. As congregational conductors, our task is to orient their trumpets of praise in the direction of the Worker who is worthy of all our praise. By reminding our people of the tremendous works of God in their daily lives, worship reorients workers and helps them put their own accomplishments in their proper place (read the verses that surround Psalm 104:23).

Second, when planned with creativity and care, Sunday morning can be a place where workers learn to carry their very specific workplace victories before the Lord in praise. Modern praise songs are often very vague and generic. Worshipers sing of God's general greatness and goodness. By design, the language of these songs is often very broad, universal, and inclusive of a broad swath of the human experience. To be clear, *there is nothing wrong with these more generic songs of praise*. The church has good reason for using these songs. That said, workers enter worship with very specific victories. Their unique and idiosyncratic workplace trumpets need to be blown. This is where skillful pastors and worship leaders come in. With a little bit of imagination, you can create spaces for worshipers to pick up their instrument and play it with all their heart.

Here are some conductor tips.

Reorientation and Remembering

How do we help workers reorient their trumpets away from themselves? We can invite them to *remember* and then, immediately afterward, we can invite them to *praise*. Psalm 77 provides us this framework by calling God's people to remember:

> I will remember the deeds of the LORD;
>   yes, I will remember your miracles of long ago.
> I will consider all your works
>   and meditate on all your mighty deeds. (vv. 11–12)

And then praise:

> Your ways, God, are holy.
>   What god is as great as our God? (v. 13)

Psalm 77 calls God's people to remember his works before praising him for all he has done for them. You can do this with a ritual similar to the song framing practice from the previous chapter. Before singing one of your more generic praise songs, offer your congregation one minute of vocational silence (this may be a gift they've not yet offered themselves). Ask them to take that minute to consider God's movement within their own calling or workplace over the past year. Invite them to remember a particular moment of vocational success, a career victory that God has clearly won for them—something that, without God, would not have come to pass. Once the minute is over, instruct them to enter the song of praise carrying that specific victory with them. The specificity of this "vocational minute" will give the praise song new life. You are, in essence, inviting them to bring their unique trumpet into the orchestra.

Example: God has gathered us for worship, and we respond with praise. As we prepare to offer up our praise and thanksgiving, I invite you to think through your last week. What moments bring you great joy? What are you proud of accomplishing? What successes have you experienced in your work and daily living? Remember with gratitude and give thanks.

[Silence]

God is good and worthy of all our praise. For God has been at work in our world and in our very lives. He has worked in us, through us, and with us. Praise God from whom all these blessings flow. Please join me as we offer up our praise.

Try scripting your own invitation to vocational silence, followed by an invitation to praise.

Remembrance: _____

_____

_____

_____

_____

[Silence]

Invitation: _____

_____

_____

_____

Reflecting and Responding

Another idea is to give your congregation an opportunity to remember, reflect on, and then voice their own trumpets of praise. If your people are comfortable with times of sharing and testimony, consider allowing people to briefly voice their own vocational words of praise, interspersed with a spoken or sung refrain. If public sharing is not yet comfortable, invite them to fill out small cards on their way in to worship. Have a leader read them, interspersing them with a spoken or sung refrain.

Example 1 (read by individuals offering their own trumpets):

This week I finished grading papers and was able to meet with the one student I was deeply concerned about.

The Lord has done great things for us, and we are filled with joy. (Ps. 126:3)

I took my elderly parents to multiple doctors' appointments and was able to be an advocate for their physical and mental health.

The Lord has done great things for us, and we are filled with joy. (Ps. 126:3)

I got to be in the spelling bee at school and made it to the final round.

The Lord has done great things for us, and we are filled with joy. (Ps. 126:3)

I delivered a package filled with medical supplies to a family with a new diagnosis. I got it there safely and in a timely manner.

The Lord has done great things for us, and we are filled with joy. (Ps. 126:3)

Example 2 (corporate, offered by a leader on behalf of the people):

God, we praise you for the work of our educators and teachers. Through them, the minds of all ages are expanded to know something new and wonderful about your world each day. Through their labor we know:

Invitation to Praise from Psalm 103

Children of God, we are gathered at the gracious invitation of God, who is our Creator, our Sustainer, and the Giver of all good gifts. God welcomes us and receives our prayers and praises, our worship and work. God delights in what we have created with our hands, engineered in our minds, and offered up in our hearts. God delights in our voices, so let us raise them up in gratitude and praise.

> Bless the Lord, my soul.
> **All my inmost being bless God's holy name.**
> God of bounty, God of goodness,
> **We praise you for your abundant gifts.**
> God of plenty, God of grace,
> **We offer you the works of our hands.**
>
> Bless the Lord, my soul.
> **Forget not all God's benefits.**
> From fields and farms, cubicles and courtrooms,
> **God delights in our offering of work.**
> So bring your treasures, the fruits of your labor,
> **Receive them, O God, as our thankful offering of praise.**
>
> Bless the Lord, my soul.
> **Bless God's holy name.**

How wide and long and high and deep is the love of Christ. (Eph. 3:18)

We praise you for our farmers, grocers, and all those who work in the food industry. Through them, we are blessed with the daily gifts of nutrition and flavor. Because of the gifts and wisdom you have given them, our families are nourished and blessed. Through their labor we know:

How wide and long and high and deep is the love of Christ. (Eph. 3:18)

We praise you for our entrepreneurs. Through them, our city is blessed with creative ideas, products, and services. Because of the gifts and wisdom you have given them, people are served, new jobs are created, and our city flourishes. Through their labor we know:

How wide and long and high and deep is the love of Christ. (Eph. 3:18)

God, we praise you for our stay-at-home parents. Through them, you care for the young and the old alike. You bless them in their many tasks, both seen and largely unseen. You work through them to bless their homes, their communities, and your world. Through their labor we know:

How wide and long and high and deep is the love of Christ. (Eph. 3:18)

Jot down a few notes below about how you might be able to incorporate this practice into your congregation's worship.

_____

_____

_____

_____

_____

Reframing Vocational Trumpets

Prayer and worship are not monologues—they are always offered to the living God who responds with delight and faithfulness. Think about what address for God you typically use to start your prayers (e.g., God, Father, Lord, Savior). Incorporating new addresses for God can help workers see God's action in the world, in their particular vocation.

Examples

God, you are Creator of all things beautiful,
we praise you for the beauty of architecture, artwork, and graphic design.

Bread of Life,
we praise you for feeding and nourishing us each day—for equipping the farmers that grow, the hands that prepare, and the mouths that receive your sustenance and care.

God our Deliverer,
we praise you for the ways in which you deliver us from danger through the work of EMTs, firefighters, and security officers.

Think about some of the main professions in your congregation and try a few praise openings of your own.

1. _____

2. _____

3. _____

Are there seasonal touchpoints you might want to remember? For example, farmers at harvest or planting, administrative assistants on Administrative Professionals Day, accountants on tax day. Write down a few and craft an opening of praise with these professions in mind.

1. _____

2. _____

Note that later you'll be making a vocational prayer calendar, and these will come in handy!

Psalms of Praise

Many of the openings of our worship services feature Scripture, particularly the psalms. The lyrics of the psalms are filled with workplace images, questions, and issues. They have a unique ability to directly engage vocational longings of workers. Whether your people are farmers or masonry experts, executives or volunteers, the Psalter contains all we need to converse with God about our trumpets of praise, our thanksgivings, victories, and wonders.[1] In the meantime, here are some comments and suggestions for use of the psalms to help orient a worker's trumpets of praise.

1. The psalms are a deep well from which we as pastors and worship leaders can draw week after week. They speak to every human emotion, offering us words and prayers for every circumstance of life. We want these words on workers' lips as they head out the door on Monday to engage their daily callings. Sadly, our use of the psalms in worship tends to be limited. We perform "psalm-ectomies," including only our favorite parts of our favorite psalms, while the rest of the book goes largely unused in corporate worship. Regular use of the psalms will broaden the worker's vocationally conversant language skills. It will not only show them how to hold their trumpets but also expand their repertoire of what they are able to play. Using the psalms is a simple (yet profound) way to lead worship for workers!

2. The psalms help workers learn how to trumpet with and for one another. A prayer for medical professionals might seem irrelevant to the magazine editor, who wonders why this matters and what it has to do with them. But with gradual reorientation, workers begin to understand that when we pray with one another, we do so as a part of a larger community of Christ that shares in one another's joys and sorrows. The language of the psalms grounds our participation in worship of all times and places, teaching us to pray not only as individuals but as the corporate family of God.

---

1. For a comprehensive overview of the psalms and their intersections with vocationally conversant worship, see Matthew Kaemingk and Cory B. Willson, *Work and Worship: Reconnecting Our Labor and Liturgy* (Baker Academic, 2020).

3. As the psalms become more familiar, find creative ways to engage workers in new and fresh ways. This is not an invitation to change the words
   of Scripture; it's an encouragement to help your people understand and
   apply it to their lives through the work of the Holy Spirit. Curious what
   this might look like? See the example below of a psalm exercise for the
   familiar words of Psalm 23, inviting workers to personally reflect on
   these words of Scripture through the lens of their own vocation.

Writing in the Spirit of Psalm 23

Psalm 23	Purpose of the Phrasing	Personal Paraphrase
The Lord is my shepherd, I lack nothing.	Identifies God through the lens of our vocation/role and states the associated benefits.	
He makes me lie down in green pastures, he leads me beside quiet waters,	Carries out the metaphor in two concrete examples.	
he refreshes my soul.	Sums up the examples.	
He guides me along the right paths for his name's sake.	Looks ahead to where or how God might lead in positive ways.	
Even though I walk through the darkest valley, I will fear no evil, for you are with me; your rod and your staff, they comfort me.	Looks ahead to where or how God might lead even in difficult circumstances. Names how God is present. Names how God comforts. (Note: the language turns to second person here.)	
You prepare a table before me in the presence of my enemies.	Adjusts the metaphor in order to picture a welcome received.	
You anoint my head with oil; my cup overflows.	Pictures honor and gracious abundance.	
Surely your goodness and love will follow me all the days of my life, and I will dwell in the house of the Lord forever.	Claims the promise of a covenantal, faithful God in the language or imagery of the metaphor.	

Created by Meg Jenista Kuykendall. Used with permission.

Example

The Lord is my companion and comforter in retirement.

He helps me enjoy my later years in life.

He provides me with all I need.

He lets me rest after forty-six years of teaching.

He leads me to enjoy his creation, travel, book groups, and fellowship
  with my family and friends.

Even though I walk more slowly on the golf course, have more pain,
    and am sometimes lonely, I have no real fears,
  for you are with me.

Your rod and staff and my cane
  keep me safe and free from falling.

You shelter me from evil in the world by being with me as a perfect
  host.

You protect me from illness and disease, and I am grateful for my
  health.

My life overflows with blessings from you and others,
  and the Lord will be a guest in my home forever.[2]

2. Written by Virginia Primus. Used with permission.

7

Workers Confess

Every Sunday workers arrive with dirty hands. Whether a business owner or a homemaker, a plumber or a daycare provider, all workers stand before the Lord with weekly burdens of guilt from their time spent in the world. All week long they've participated in and contributed to a fallen and broken economy that is rebelling against the economy of God.

How might the worker's hands be washed?

How might their burdens be lifted?

The issue of a worker's "dirty hands" in a holy place of worship is as old as the Christian faith itself. The early church had a significant fight over marketplace sins in Christian worship. The earliest instructions for worship leaders argued that sinful people should not be allowed to carry their workplace offerings into worship. These restrictions included all manner of workers: gladiators, prostitutes, dishonest lawyers, sorcerers, business owners who oppressed the poor, and innkeepers who watered down their wine.[1] These workers were not allowed to bring their tainted offerings into holy worship. They were forced to quit their work and go through a period of vocational purification and reemployment before they could again join in worship.

Soon enough the early church started to ask the rather uncomfortable question, Whose hands *are* clean enough to be raised in holy worship? Whose

---

1. *Didascalia XVIII*, in *Didascalia Apostolorum: The Syriac Version*, trans. R. Hugh Connolly (Wipf & Stock, 2009), 158.

work is pure enough to make an offering to the most holy God? All have sinned and fallen short of the glory of God. All of us have been enriched by a marketplace that is in rebellion against God. How can any worker bring their sin-stained hands and profits into worship?

Rather than shrink away in despair, one theologian in the early church offered a word of Christ-centered hope and encouragement. He argued that Christ's hands can wash the worker's sin-stained hands, that Christ's work can wash their work. As the worker enters into worship, he argued, Christ can walk before and beside them. *In and through the work of Christ, our sin-stained work can be transformed into worship.* This was good news for ancient Christian workers, and it can be good news for workers today as well.

> When my work takes me places I don't want to go—Christ before me
> And my heart aches with sorrow as I hit the road—Christ be with me
>
> When the care of my family takes all that I have—Christ within me
> When I'm worn and exhausted, ashamed that I'm mad—Christ
>   defend me
>
> I rise up today in a strength that is not my own
> I'm held by the promise of God that I'm never alone
>   —"Breastplate of St Patrick" by The Porter's Gate

Confession: To Unburden the Worker

While a formal prayer of confession may strike some worship leaders as a dour ritual of guilt, shame, and sadness, it doesn't need to be so. A dedicated time of confession in worship should actually be the most joyful and liberating moment of an entire Sunday morning. Here your people are afforded the opportunity to be unburdened. You are giving them the gift of time, a period of quiet reflection in which they can honestly name their sins and experience relief. In the assurance of pardon, workers can be reminded of the forgiveness and freedom of Christ.

So, how can you lead workers into a time of confession? How might their hands be washed and their shoulders unburdened?

Whether your times of confession are scripted or unscripted, spoken or silent, they should be mindful of the diversity of guilt and shame that different people carry into the sanctuary. Some come with a sense of personal guilt and shame regarding their individual behavior in the workplace. They've been selfish or short, conceited or controlling. Others carry a more communal or corporate sort of guilt regarding their contributions to a sinful workplace culture, industry, or mode of work. They've contributed to market practices that oppress the poor, crush workers, perpetuate racism, and feed off the worst human instincts.

It will be important for your times of confession to attend to both the personal and the corporate nature of sin in the world. Sometimes we need to confess our personal sins; other times we need to confess our participation in sinful systems and structures. Both matter. After all, Christ "comes to make his blessings flow far as the curse is found."

What distinguishes a time of confession from a time of lament is the question of agency and responsibility. In lament, workers weep over things they can't control. They name the sinful destruction they witness but are powerless to stop. They have no agency or responsibility. In confession, on the other hand, workers weep over the shameful things *they themselves* have done or left undone. We are not always the victims of larger systems; sometimes we are the culprits. However small we are, workers have power and agency in the marketplace. Our behavior should reflect this. Naming our culpability in larger systems of destruction is a way of naming our sacred responsibility.

One point of clarity on this matter. While lament and confession are distinct actions, they can overlap. For example, what might begin as an isolated sin for a worker (worthy of confession) might become a sinful pattern and later a sinful prison (worthy of lament). The worker may have started with agency and responsibility at the beginning, but as their sin grew, it overtook them and imprisoned them. While confession was appropriate at the beginning, they are now in a state of lament. As Paul wrote, "I do not understand what I do. For what I want to do I do not do, but what I hate I do" (Rom. 7:15). In confession, the worker can cry, "God, where are you? Why have you not yet released me from this prison I have made?"

Some workers might have an individualistic understanding of sin as being personally selfish, mean, or impatient but have no understanding of the corporate nature of sin as a virus that also infects the structures of our working lives in the forms of structural sexism, greed, and racism. Attending to the complex personal and public nature of sin is important.

Prayer of Confession Adapted from the Book of Common Prayer

Most merciful God, we confess that we have sinned against you in thought, word, and deed, by what we have done and by what we have left undone.

Our sins, O God, are great. We personally confess what we have done and left undone in our places of work and daily living. We also confess that we have intentionally and unintentionally participated in broken systems of greed, selfish gain, and destruction. Our hands have participated in personal and corporate ways. Forgive us.

We have not loved you with our whole heart; we have not loved our neighbors as ourselves. We are truly sorry and we humbly repent.

We call to mind those we have mistreated: the harsh words said, the poor decisions we have made against our neighbor. We also remember that through our action and inaction, we have contributed to the marginalization of the poor and vulnerable. Forgive us.

For the sake of your Son Jesus Christ, have mercy on us and forgive us; that we may delight in your will, and walk in your ways, to the glory of your name. Amen.

In toxic workplaces, it can be extremely rare to hear a leader confess, "I was wrong, I hurt you, and I apologize. Will you forgive me? I want to do better." Through a formal ritual of confession, workers can be gradually formed to enter their workplaces practicing this new and uncomfortable language of humility and contrition.

As you might expect, an employee who quickly admits their faults, seeks forgiveness, and works for repair is a strange creature in a cutthroat workplace. Such a figure is liable to pique their colleagues' curiosity.

Your congregation's unique style and approach to confession will differ from those of other congregations. Style is not our immediate concern. There

Prayer of Confession
for Those Who Cannot Slow Down

I confess I have used every excuse, telling myself everything I
need to hear.
I have convinced myself those extra hours in front of my screen
are a virtue.
I have judged those around me, measuring their output against
my unsustainable pace.

I confess I enjoy working myself sick; mind, body, and spirit.
My productivity has taken the place of peace.
My life is slipping by, and people are slipping through the
cracks.

I confess I don't know how else to live.
I love the rat race, and knowing how busy I am.
I hold my identity in my impossibly long to-do list.

I confess I need you, as much as I want to do it on my own.
I need you, when I think you move too slow for my fast pace.
I need you, behind me, beneath me, before me.

Written by Kristy Bootsma. Used with permission.

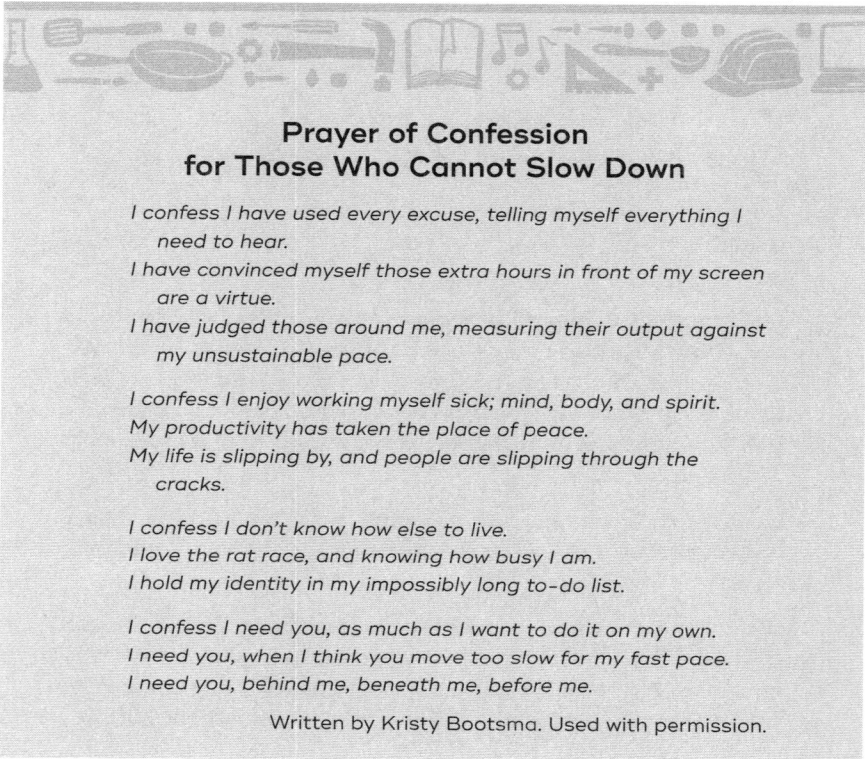

are, however, a few key ingredients that can deepen your time of confession in a vocationally conversant way. For our purposes, it might be helpful to break the time of confession down into four distinct parts.

1. **Personal Confession:** Workers are invited to examine their week and their hands, acknowledging the grime and grit that cover them. This is a self-directed time of quiet and personal reflection. Individuals are responsible for finding and naming the burdens that need to be lifted.

2. **Corporate Confession:** Here a worship leader helps congregants collectively recognize and name sins they might not have noticed on their own. Workplace evils are sometimes subtle and hidden, complicated and deep. Sometimes we cannot see the complex ways in which we are mired in the grasp of evil. In a time of corporate confession, a leader or a script can uncover aspects of our workplace guilt that we might have trouble recognizing or naming.

3. **Assurance of Pardon:** God graciously responds to a worshiper's confession with words of forgiveness and pardon. Here the leader makes the joyful announcement that, through the work of Christ, the worker's hands have been cleaned. This should be a celebrative moment in worship. Workers are united to Christ and free to work *in him*.

4. **Invitation to a Grace-Based Life:** We respond to Christ's work of grace with a new kind of work in the world: one that is grace-based. As we look down at our clean hands, our first impulse is to put them to work in gracious acts of service for others. Christ has done a great work on our behalf, and so we go in peace to work on behalf of others rather than ourselves alone.

All worshiping contexts are different. Whether you use our four-part structure or not, be sure that both God and the congregants are active agents in your time of confession. Together workers and their God should engage in a transformative dialogue that includes both brutal truth telling and overwhelming grace. Always be sure that your times of honest truth telling are nestled within the safety and security of God's gracious activity that is radically with and for your people. Your people should confess with the assurance that God responds graciously to their confessions.

Keeping with our fourfold structure, consider some of the following examples as models for your congregation's approach to confession.

Call to Personal Confession

There are many Scripture passages that invite a worker to examine themselves to see where they have been sinful and participated within sinful systems (Pss. 32; 66; 139; Isa. 1:18; Heb. 4:14–16; 9:19–23; James 5:16; 1 John 1:5–9; 2:1–2). Anchor a call to confession in Scripture and invite a silent reflection of sin.

Example: As we prepare to pray to God and offer up our confession of sin, we remember the words of the psalmist, who says,

> You have searched me, LORD,
>   and you know me.

You know when I sit and when I rise;
>   you perceive my thoughts from afar. (Ps. 139:1–2)

In these moments of silence, we look at our hands and think about what they have done and left undone this week. In the same way, we look into our hearts and, just as God has searched us and known us, we call these things to mind.

[Silence]

Search me, God, and know my heart;
>   test me and know my anxious thoughts.
See if there is any offensive way in me,
>   and lead me in the way everlasting. (Ps. 139:23–24)

Let us pray.

Corporate Prayer of Confession

There is no "right way" to offer a confession. In fact, trying different forms of confession will keep this moment in your service from becoming lip service. Consider some of the following ideas. Rely heavily on silence.

Merciful God, we confess the many ways we have sinned against you. We think about those things we have done intentionally or unintentionally, those sins we have done that are known to others and those known only to you. Hear our silent prayers.

>   [Silence]

We confess the sins we have committed against our neighbors, our colleagues, our friends, and our family.

>   [Silence]

We confess our participation in broken and sinful systems like our places of work, our communities, and our homes.

>   [Silence]

Hear our prayer, O Lord. Amen.

Confession from the Theology of Work Project

*Let us be assured of God's power to relieve sin, to take away
  our burden and debt.
We bring before you, Lord, all the failure of our daily work;
we have fallen short of your demands upon us;
we have not given you the glory, nor worked in your love.*

Good Lord, forgive us:
Forgive us, Lord.

*We confess the faults of the industrial society in which we work,
the inequalities, the injustices of all systems
and the difficulties we have in changing them.*

Good Lord, forgive us:
Forgive us, Lord.

*We have not worked together as brothers and sisters of your
  family.
There have been differences, lack of cooperation and chances
  of reconciliation missed.
We have not brought out the best in others.*

Good Lord, forgive us:
Forgive us, Lord.

*We have wasted and misused the raw materials of the earth,
and scarred the beauty of nature.
We have not made best use of the time and skills you have
  given us.
Good Lord, forgive us:*
Forgive us, Lord.

*We have not met the needs of the hungry and impoverished of
  the world.
We have not been able to meet the demands of those without
  work.*

Good Lord, forgive us:
Forgive us, Lord. Amen.

"We Bring Before You, Lord, All the Failures of Our Daily Work," Theology of
Work Project, accessed January 31, 2025, https://www.theologyofwork.org
/book/work-in-worship/prayer-material-for-services/confession/we-bring
-before-you-lord-all-the-failures-of-our-daily-work-prayer/.

Prayer Writing Exercise

If you have extended time in a worship service or a retreat to focus on the practice of confession, consider the following exercise. Here you can help your flock pray using a series of concentric circles, pondering the unique forms of sin in their working life. Invite them to write or silently pray their confessions for each circle.

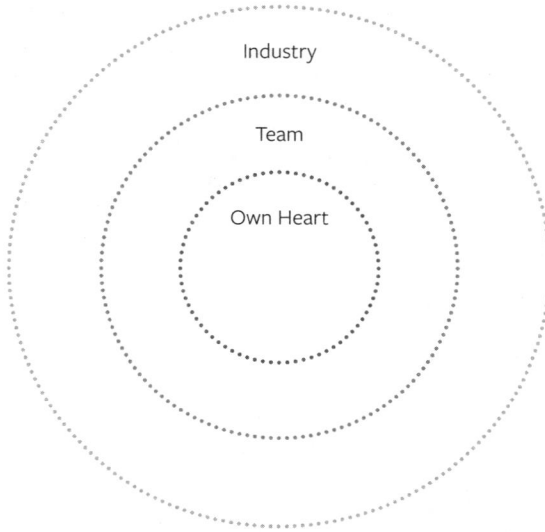

- **Outermost Ring**
  Think about your particular industry or calling (e.g., medicine, real estate, sales, stay-at-home mom, mechanic, and retiree). Consider how your industry or calling falls prey to unique injustices, temptations, evils, and vices. Take some time to name your own complicity in these evils. Confess the ways in which you participate in the brokenness of your industry's culture.

- **Middle Ring**
  Now zoom down. Think about your team of colleagues. This is the closest group of people you work with and serve alongside on a daily basis. Your team has developed a little culture for itself—a way of serving alongside one another. Take a moment and consider the various ways in which the working culture and dynamics of your team have grown

misshapen because of sin and evil. Rather than blame your team, name your own complicity in the team's dysfunction. Take some time to confess the ways in which you personally contribute to the brokenness of your particular circle.

- **Inner Ring**
  In the other rings, you are guilty of "going with the flow." In this circle, you are naming the ways in which you carry your own unique vices into the workplace. Here you consider the interior machinations of your own heart. Consider your own internal vices, fears, temptations, and bad habits that you carry into the workplace. Take some time to name and confess the ways in which you personally need Christ to convict and transform your own heart this week. Be specific.

This would be a powerful exercise to do with a small group but could also be done in corporate worship.

- Include a picture of the concentric circles on your projection screen. Walk your people through these circles of prayer, leaving generous space for silent prayer and confession.
- You can also hand out a piece of paper with the concentric circles and invite people to write various words and phrases. At the appropriate time, congregants can carry their confessions forward and drop them in a (secure) box. A word of comfort, encouragement, and pardon should quickly follow.
- Concentric circles can also be sent home with people to leave on their desk or in another prominent location. Here the visual serves as a prompt to pause, meditate, and pray.

Assurance of Pardon

Prayers of confession are immediately followed by God's words of pardon and grace. These can be as simple as declaring, "Children of God, take heart. Through the work of Christ your sins are forgiven." These words are not magical. They are naming a reality that is already true—in Christ, we have been forgiven, we are loved, and we are accepted and freed.

Example: In all the ways our work falls short, the work of Christ graciously covers us with words of assurance and grace. "In him we have redemption through his blood, the forgiveness of sins, in accordance with the riches of God's grace that he lavished on us" (Eph. 1:7–8). Christ is at work within you. Amen.

Invitation to a Grace–Based Life

How can I say thanks for the things you have done for me?
Things so undeserved yet you give to prove your love for me.
The voices of a million angels could not express my gratitude.
All that I am and ever hope to be, I owe it all to thee.[2]

How should a worker respond to the forgiveness and grace they have received? They should get back to work! Forgiveness is not a static declaration that leaves a worker unchanged. Rather, it is the impetus that propels them back into God's world filled with joy, gratitude, and resolve. In this transformative dialogue God says, "You are forgiven!" God's people must respond by saying, "Thank you."

There are countless verses in Scripture that invite workers to live in grace-filled ways toward God and their neighbor. A simple framing of these verses reminds workers that God's forgiveness should have consequences in the local community.

Example 1: As those who have been forgiven, the dirty garments of our sin have been removed. We are now sent back into our places of work and daily living clothed with the garments of Christ. Hear these words, and remember them this week as you share God's grace with all you encounter.

Therefore, as God's chosen people, holy and dearly loved, clothe yourselves with compassion, kindness, humility, gentleness and patience. Bear with each other and forgive one another if any of you has a grievance against someone. Forgive as the Lord forgave you. And over all these virtues put on love, which binds them all together in perfect unity. (Col. 3:12–14)

Example 2: The Lord has been so good to us, forgiving our sins and declaring that in Christ we have been set free. Psalm 116:12–14 asks, "What shall

---

2. Written by Andre Crouch. Copyright © 1971 Bud John Songs. All rights reserved. Used with permission.

I return to the LORD for all his goodness to me?" The psalmist says, "Lift up the cup of salvation and call on the name of the LORD. I will fulfill my vows to the LORD in the presence of all his people." In the work that God calls you to this week, remember your forgiveness—the cup of salvation, the gift of Christ. Fulfill your vows of gratitude and holy living. Live and work in a way that all who see and know you might come to recognize the goodness of God.

8

Workers Lament

When the weight bears down on me
And it's more than I can hold
Won't you take it and lift it on your shoulders
You're not a stranger to the heavy load

—"Not a Stranger" by The Porter's Gate

Working in a broken world can produce a multitude of tears. There are thorns and thistles in the fields of the Lord, and they can leave deep scars. Each Sunday men and women stumble into the sanctuary bearing a variety of wounds, heartbreaks, and laments. Feeling frustrated, exhausted, broken, and—worst of all—completely powerless, they sit in the pew silently stewing. Like the Israelites laboring under Pharaoh, today's workers are often asked to make more bricks with less straw (Exod. 5:6–9). They endure surprise layoffs, cruel bosses, unsafe working conditions, and the constant threat of "rightsizing." Navigating dead-end jobs, volatile workplaces, and unjust pay, workers enter the sanctuary asking, "Are my tears welcome here?"

Many of today's worship services are completely bereft of the language of lament. In these sanctuaries, worshipers are well trained in expressions of joy, gratitude, and praise. They artfully use positive spiritual language to bless and commission, present offerings, and even confess their sins. But when it comes to expressing words of lament and prayers of painful longing, they might as well be speaking a foreign language. *No tears allowed.*

Some churches are well versed in shedding empathetic tears and offering heartfelt thoughts and prayers for the suffering of others. They can address other people's laments with fluency. But when it comes time to honestly examine their own, their prayer skills fall short. Being good students of Scripture, people in these congregations know the right psalms to turn to when national tragedies or health crises strike. God might care about a cancer diagnosis or natural disaster, but can I—*should I?*—bother the almighty God of the universe with my (seemingly mundane) workplace issues?

Workers in these congregations will need to learn a new language: *the language of lament.* Like all foreign tongues, it will need to be practiced. After all, we can't become fluent in a language we never hear or practice.

As they stumble and practice, your people will gradually learn that they can, in fact, be honest with God about their daily work, not simply because he allows it but because he lovingly welcomes it. Thankfully, God is not simply with us when we celebrate; he is with us when we weep as well. The very first thing the Israelites learned about their God was that they could cry out about their work. This God would draw near to them and respond to their workplace tears. Their forefather Jacob learned intimately that to wrestle with God is to know him. Jacob's new name, Israel, means quite literally "the one who wrestles with God."

As your people develop a fluency in the language of lament, they will begin to learn to wrestle with God about their daily work. In doing so, a delightful side effect may come into play: They will begin to develop deeper levels of authenticity and vulnerability with one another. In time you may find that your sanctuary becomes a place where tears are welcome after all.

In the sanctuary, we have the sensitive and sacred opportunity to train our people in the language of lament. No doubt, this is a language some of them will need (and use) all week long. The sacred task of the worship leader is to guide your people in telling the truth about the weight they carry and the scars they bear. This can happen corporately in more generalized prayers of lament, but it can also happen individually, either out loud or in guided times of silent reflection.

To build your congregation's fluency in the language of lament, you can provide several different ways of expressing workplace pain and groaning. Try different forms of prayer to engage workers in various seasons of lament.

Congregational Prayer Exercises

A prayer of lament normally has four distinct parts. Each plays an important role.

1. **An Address:** Just as a worker's trumpet of praise must be blown toward God, so too their tears of lament must be cried *toward* God. This is not an aimless complaint that will be shouted into the darkness; we have an audience with the living God. This is a deeply personal and relational lament, demonstrating a high level of trust in the One who receives it. Focus the congregation's cries toward God directly.

   Example: "Jesus, we know that you wept in the face of great loss. We bring our tears to you today . . ."

2. **A Complaint:** After addressing God, the worshiper names their complaint. Nothing held back. Nothing polished or well articulated. Here the worker can express everything from anger, to sadness, to confusion. They lament that which they experience personally and that which they witness globally. There are no rules for this complaint. Let loose. We ask only that you honor God by directing your complaints to him.

   Example: "This terrible _____ is happening. Where are you? Why is this happening? When will you put a stop to this? We don't understand!"

3. **A Request:** A lament expects an answer. It seeks more than mere expression. When workers hurl their complaints to God, they have an expectation that he is going to do something about them. This request can come in the form of a plea, a question, a demand, or simply an ask.

   Examples: "Hear us, God, and respond." "Come quickly, God." "Make your justice known." "Do not stay silent."

4. **A Declaration of Trust:** Many psalms of lament end with a declaration of trust (but not all!). A declaration of trust can help people remember and reorient themselves once again to God's long history of faithfulness and trustworthiness. This is not an assumption that this particular complaint will be answered in the way they have asked; it's trusting that God hears and will continue to be faithful.

   Example: "We know that you have been faithful in the past with _____, and we trust that in your mercy _____. Help us to see your will and your wisdom. Help us to seek your glory, whatever your plan might be."

This fourfold structure may prove useful for writing both personal and congregational prayers of lament. In the space below, begin practicing your own fluency in the language of lament and write a personal prayer about your work. Be specific to your own life.

Address: _____

_____

_____

Complaint: _____

_____

_____

Request: _____

_____

_____

Declaration of Trust: _____

_____

_____

Now try a more generic prayer of lament with workers in mind that could be used in congregational worship.

Address: _____

_____

_____

Complaint: _____

_____

_____

Request: _____

_____

_____

Declaration of Trust: _____

_____

_____

Prayer of Lament

God of heaven and earth.
Another receives credit for my industry.
My boss overlooks me.
I am tossed aside.
Swapped for someone younger or cheaper or well-connected.

I am spread thin. I am worn and weary.
Exhausted. Spent. And ashamed.
Threadbare, I rise each morning indentured to this—
forced into soulless and soul-numbing work, to eke out a dreary living.

On my bed, I dream of work,
At night my labor haunts me.
It is all sorrow and frustration.
Meaningless. Meaningless. Everything is meaningless.

The cynic is right. What does anyone gain from all their slog and sweat?
Why waste our days toiling?
Generations come and generations go.
The wind blows round and round.
Water evaporates only to rain and evaporate again.
Our work swirls like liquid down a drain. What can it matter?
Meaningless. Meaningless. Everything is meaningless.

Yet
you rekindle our faith.
Remind us that in you and through you all work matters.
Stir us to "Do everything in love."
Save us. And we can give ourselves fully to your work.
Because in you, our labor is not in vain.
Amen.[1]

---

1. Written by Kevin Adams. Used with permission.

Fluency Builders

The creative use of brief refrains is a tried-and-true method of developing a fluency in the language of lament. Throughout its history, Christianity has leaned heavily on a variety of short, simple refrains that people can easily repeat and rehearse in times of trouble. These short phrases function like spiritual "anchors" in the storms of life. When an individual has no words to describe their pain, these phrases fill the void. These refrains are an easy way for a worker to offer up their laments to God in their daily life and work. Here are some common refrains:

- Come quickly, Lord.
- How long, O Lord?
- Holy God, have mercy on us.
- Lord, in your mercy, hear our prayer.
- Lord, have mercy. Christ, have mercy. (*Kyrie eleison. Christe eleison.*)

How might you use a short spoken refrain to help guide your congregation in a prayer of lament? Try scripting a short prayer using one of the above refrains or one of your own.

Example 1

Leader: All creation groans. Natural disasters wreak havoc on land and lives. Our inability to use less means a high cost for those most vulnerable among us. What you created as good is marred by the work of our hands.

People: Come quickly, Lord.

Leader: Wars rage around the globe. Our prayers and our work feel help-less and sometimes hopeless in the face of violent death, displaced people, and perpetual conflict.

People: Come quickly, Lord.

Leader: Our communities suffer. We see the effects of poverty, inequality, addiction, and abuse all around us. Some of us experience this personally. It may be known here by others, and it may be known only to you.

People: Come quickly, Lord.

Leader: We struggle in our daily work. In our offices, our stores, our fields, our homes—wherever we go each day—we lament the struggle and the pain we face.

People: Come quickly, Lord. Amen.

Example 2

Leader: Lord our God, there is an abundance of suffering in our world, and we sometimes wonder, Are you even paying attention?

To abandoned and neglected children?

To the elderly who are lonely for family or friends?

To the invisible poor, the homeless?

To those devastated by natural disasters and the results of environmental degradation?

To those raised in the church and near to our hearts who now live their own way without looking back?

People: Lord, have mercy. Christ, have mercy.

Leader: Lord our God, there is an abundance of suffering in our world, and we sometimes wonder, Are you ever going to step in and fix this?

The despair and anxiety of mental illness.

The shame, regrets, and grief that plague us in the day and steal our sleep at night.

The persecution of the weak by the strong, the poor by the rich, the powerless by those in power.

The temptation, sin, and addiction that diminish us and destroy our relationships.

People: Lord, have mercy. Christ, have mercy.

Leader: Lord our God, there is an abundance of suffering in our world, and we sometimes wonder, Where exactly is your kingdom of justice and peace?

We don't see it in racism and acts of hate against one another.

We don't see it in careless speech, in trolls and bullying on the internet, in our politics and on our playgrounds.

We don't see it in churches and Christians who prefer silence, a peace that is nothing more than the absence of conflict or cheap grace to the work of justice.

We don't see it in ourselves, in our families, in our communities. Where are you? Is your kingdom really on the way?

People: Lord, have mercy. Christ, have mercy.

Leader: When we are angry, remind us of your past faithfulness.

When we are angry, show us your present love and salvation.

When we are angry, turn us toward humility, courageous hope, and gentle persistence.

Turn us to you, the only One who has ever managed to turn anger into forgiveness, wrath into salvation, and outrage into healing and who will one day turn all this world toward righteousness, justice, and peace.

People: Lord, have mercy. Christ, have mercy.

Amen.

Creative Prayer Exercises

Why?

Children are experts at asking "why" questions. "Why did my friend move away?" "Why can't I have another dessert?" "Why did Grandma get sick and die?" They feel the freedom, curiosity, and safety to persist with their parents by asking "Why?" Children of God are free and safe to ask God "why" in the same way, even when no answer will suffice. Below, practice writing a very simple "why" prayer. With a particular vocational situation in mind, write a prayer asking several questions. Feel safe and free to ask questions that don't necessarily have an answer.

Dear God,

I trust that you are listening. So, hear my prayer about my vocation.

Why _____

_____

Why _____

_____

Why _____

_____

Please listen and answer me. Amen.

Tears

Trace and cut small teardrop shapes out of paper or cardstock. Distribute them and invite people to write a single word or a short phrase that represents their vocational tears. This could be a set of tears stemming from their school, workplace, or a place of service in the home or community. As people are able, have them carry their teardrops forward and offer them up in prayer. You could collect them in a clear glass jar so they can be seen. People could hang them on a piece of fabric. This could be a one-off or you could choose to build on this display for a season. For obvious reasons, some people might not want to make their tears public. Limiting ourselves to writing a single word or phrase can offer a way for worshipers to share without oversharing.

Prayer Exercises

Two different kinds of congregational prayer can be particularly helpful in articulating our laments to God. Developed by the followers of Ignatius of Loyola, these two modes of prayer are called "kataphatic" and "apophatic." Kataphatic prayers give the congregation specific words and ideas, while apophatic prayers create an open space for spontaneous words and ideas to emerge within the congregation organically. Both forms of prayer offer powerful potential for leading prayers of lament.

Kataphatic Prayer

Kataphatic prayer can offer speechless workers the words and phrases they so desperately need to speak with God about their daily life and work. In times of workplace difficulty, people struggle to find the words they need to talk to God about their tears. Kataphatic prayers like Psalm 13 resonate with them and can be used in their own laments toward God. Cries like "How long, Lord?" and "Look on me!" and "Answer!"

With a specific worker in mind (maybe you!), write a prayer of lament based on Psalm 13. Fill in the blanks below.

How long, Lord, will _____? How long will you forget and hide
your face from _____? How long will we _____ and day

after day have _____ in our hearts? How long will _____ triumph over me? Look on me and answer! Give light to my eyes or I will sleep in death and_____ will say _____. But I trust in your unfailing love and rejoice in your salvation in _____. I will sing the Lord's praise, for he has been good to me through _____.

Apophatic Prayer

Apophatic prayers, on the other hand, are wordless and content-free. They are all blank spaces. These prayers invite workers into the uncomfortable but transformative space of open contemplation. Apophatic prayers are more challenging, but this can make them all the more potent. With the same worker in mind, imagine how you might use Psalm 13 to create an open and apophatic time of prayer during congregational worship. Consider the following breath prayer in which congregation members can carry their specific tears from their week of service in work, school, or some other sector.

Breath Prayer

[Name a daily lament.] (Inhale.) *How long, O Lord?* (Exhale.)
[Name a daily lament.] (Inhale.) *How long, O Lord?* (Exhale.)
[Name a daily lament.] (Inhale.) *Look on me.* (Exhale.)
[Name a daily lament.] (Inhale.) *Answer.* (Exhale.)

In apophatic prayer, the worker must practice silently breathing and waiting on the Lord, tears in hand.

Sometimes there simply are no words at all. The pain is something we carry in our bodies; it's buried deep in our bones. The following hand exercise can help your people access their weekly laments and slowly begin to offer them to God. No words necessary.

Posture Prayer

Close your eyes.
Consider a chronic pain or frustration in your daily life and labor.
Hold your fists tightly as you share your anger and impatience with God.
Shake your hands as you express your sadness and exhaustion with God.
Slowly open your hands as you commit these tears to God's will.

A Lament for the Unemployed

Unemployed . . . redundant . . . laid off . . . unqualified . . . surplus labor.

These words cut into me, severing all feeling of usefulness.
What kind of body-part am I now?
What sort of foot or hand, eye or ear, can I be if I don't work?
Does the body still need me?

Creator God,
I've got this idea I must be active and busy,
doing big things in your name;
prophesying to the world,
eradicating poverty.
Yet it is the everyday struggles
that can be so demanding:
just about making ends meet,
maintaining some dignity.
I might not have been the greatest worker
but now I've been put on the scrap heap.

Teacher Christ,
We need to learn a new way of being.
Show us how to be prophets in every situation,
Employed or unemployed,
Underpaid or overworked,
so that the justice of labor shared
may truly build up your body
in honor and rejoicing.

Janet Lees and Bob Warwicker, "A Lament for the Unemployed," Theology of Work Project, accessed July 20, 2025, https://www.theologyofwork.org/book/work-in-worship/private-prayer/. Used with permission.

9

Workers Listen

A young waitress sits in the pew, doing her best to pay attention to your sermon. But it's hard. She can't concentrate. The cooks in her restaurant have been fighting viciously all week. Her boss cut her hours. One of the other waiters has started making racist jokes about the dishwasher.

She wants to listen to the sermon. She wants to hear what you have to say. She prays, "God, help me to focus; help me to hear your Word." Through sheer force of will, the waitress manages to suppress all her workplace frustrations and concerns. But her success is fleeting. No matter how hard she tries, she can't remain present. Her body might be in the pew, but her heart is back at the restaurant.

Work can be captivating. Some workers absolutely love their jobs. The exciting projects and challenges capture their imagination and just won't let go. For this waitress, however, work's entrancing power is both dark and troubling. For good or ill, workplace thoughts will often win out over a sermon.

While there's nothing a preacher can do to stop these workplace intrusions, they can be powerfully reframed. Rather than seeing them as sinful distractions or evidence of spiritual immaturity, pastors can invite their people to reorient these moments as prompts to prayer and contemplation. Don't suppress workplace longings and laments; bring them into the sanctuary and into this particular sermon. Perhaps the Holy Spirit is prompting the waitress to do what she should have done at the beginning of worship. *"Daughter, offer your concerns and lay them down before me. Don't hold back."*

Reframed in this way, the sermon is no longer an escape—it's an engagement. Rather than a pastoral monologue she passively receives or consumes, the sermon becomes an active dialogue, a conversation with God that can last all week. Rather than feeling guilty about her "failure" to keep the restaurant out of your perfectly crafted sermon, the waitress can actually carry herself and her coworkers into the word that God is speaking.

In the pages that follow, we want to explore how your sermon might become less of an individual event and more of a team sport—one that *includes* the waitress and her workplace, Scripture and the Spirit. If workers are not actively bringing themselves and their lives to the sermon, it remains incomplete. In this sense, a sermon is not "finished" in the preacher's office. That's where it begins. A sermon is something that pastors and people "make" together through the power of the Spirit and the direction of the Word. You're not alone in the pulpit; the people are partnering in something with you.

"All Scripture is God-breathed and is useful for teaching, rebuking, correcting and training in righteousness, so that the servant of God may be thoroughly equipped for every good work" (2 Tim. 3:16–17). While we believe in the transformational power of Scripture, when workers hold back, when they refuse to actively carry their careers and callings into the sermon, there is nothing for the sermon to grab on to, nothing to rebuke, correct, or train.

In this chapter, we offer preachers a number of practical ideas, resources, and principles for preaching alongside (rather than at) workers. In this team sport, each side has a responsibility that, in many ways, mirrors the other.

1. The people have to actively carry their daily lives and labor into the sermon.
2. The preachers have to actively carry the daily lives and labor of their people into their sermons.

We've already discussed the former; the remainder of the chapter explores the latter.

Why Preach About Work?

To teach like Jesus and the authors of the epistles is to search out and regularly proclaim the truth of the kingdom in the language of regular work.

—Matt Rusten, *Pastoring for Monday*

If we plan to preach the Bible—and we should—we must be prepared to preach about work. The Holy Scriptures are positively inundated with more than eight hundred references to work, including discussions of craft and calling, money and markets, farmers and fields. If you pay attention to the sermons of Jesus and the writings of the apostles, you will see that they preach about work with stunning regularity. Whenever the New Testament wants to describe the kingdom of God, it almost always uses metaphors of work and labor.[1] Out of Jesus's thirty-seven parables, thirty-two make reference to work and workers. His workplace parables refer to twenty-two different occupations.[2] When Paul, James, and Peter want to communicate a spiritual truth, each one of them reaches for a vocational or economic image to get their point across (1 Cor. 3:10; 2 Tim. 2:4–7; James 5:7; 1 Pet. 5:2). If you want to be a biblical preacher, you simply can't avoid preaching about work.

Of course, there are also practical reasons to preach about work. The people in the pews are already thinking about it during your sermon. You might as well help them frame those workplace thoughts with Scripture. Many of these workers came to church on Sunday hoping for some word of encouragement or direction for what they will be facing on Monday. They desire—they *need*—sermons that matter. They long for sermons that connect them to their calling and context through the wisdom of Scripture. They want your sermon to illuminate the text *and their lives*.

An intellectual understanding of the gospel, while helpful and necessary, is not our final goal. Ultimately, we desire a people who can *live and extend* that gospel into their communities. As preachers, our job is to come alongside them and accompany them as they carry the gospel into their work. Together with Scripture, the pastor and the people are developing a "redemptive imagination," exploring the shape and demands of the gospel in all their diverse callings and careers.

1. Matt Rusten, *Pastoring for Monday: Help Your Congregation Integrate Faith and Work*, forthcoming.
2. Klaus Issler, *Living into the Life of Jesus: The Formation of Christian Character* (Inter-Varsity, 2012).

Preaching on Work Requires Pastoral Credibility and Confidence

Jesus spent the majority of his life working, not preaching. We know precious little about his craft, but we know that Jesus worked long and hard hours for meager wages. We know almost nothing about his appearance, but we can say—with great confidence—that his hands were calloused. When the time finally came for the carpenter to stand up in front of the crowds and preach the gospel, he did so with rough hands, a weathered face, and a strong back. His many sermons about work and workers were neither abstract nor theoretical; they came from a craftsman who had been there. His sermons on work had a credibility and confidence that can come only from years in the marketplace, not the temple or synagogue.

While Jesus worked for years *before* he started preaching, Paul worked for years *while* he was preaching. The famous preacher was also a skilled tentmaker who worked hard for many years alongside his congregations. It is clear that Paul viewed his identity as a worker not simply as a way to pay the bills but as a way that he might connect in a deeper and more meaningful way with Christ's people (Acts 18:2–3; 20:33–35; 1 Cor. 9:6–10; 1 Thess. 2:9; 2 Thess. 3:7–8). While some of his ministry happened in homes and synagogues, much of it happened in the marketplace as well (Acts 17:16–34). Furthermore, his preaching was not merely spiritual; it had economic consequences that got Paul in trouble with marketplace leaders more than once (Acts 16:16–24; 19:23–41).

Jesus and Paul were not detached from labor and the markets. They were experienced in buying and selling, crafting and creating, negotiating and bartering. Their years of lived experience in the markets prepared them to use workplace stories and metaphors with pastoral credibility and confidence. They knew intimately what work was like, and it clearly informed their preaching.

So, what should modern preachers do with all this information? Should they suddenly become bi-vocational? That's a debate for another book. Here we are interested in how pastors might develop the credibility and confidence they need to make a meaningful connection with workers through their sermons. When you stand up to discuss the beauty and brokenness of work, how will your people truly hear and connect with you? Below we offer seven steps that any preacher can take to make some progress on this challenge.

1. **Visit Workers**

   Make it a regular practice to get out of your church building and meet your people on their turf. Take a tour of their factories, restaurants, and offices. Taste their coffee and smell their engines, ride their elevator and listen to the music in their shop, sit in the cab of their truck and watch their heart monitors. If they are amenable, offer to pray a blessing over their workspace (see chap. 22, "Blessing Workspaces"). Being physically present in their place of work will move your sermons out of the abstract and the general, and will ground them in a raw and embodied reality. When you get up to preach on Sunday, you will have some legs to stand on.

2. **Ask Questions**

   When you visit, ask more questions and offer fewer answers. Demonstrate more than just pastoral care. Demonstrate *pastoral curiosity*. Your exploration of their workplace joys, heartaches, and testimonies will guide and enrich your preaching in untold ways. You're normally perceived as the teacher in the sanctuary, but here in the workplace the roles can be reversed to tremendous effect. Suddenly *they're* the teacher, the host, and the expert. Sitting at their table, you remember that Jesus—more often than not—was a guest at tables that did not belong to him. Like Christ, learn to ask penetrating questions, and invite them to make a theology of their work. Assuming the posture of a student, become curious and listen closely for their stories of workplace lament, confession, and transformation. The goal of workplace visits is not to harvest great sermon illustrations—though that will happen. The goal is deeper connection with workers that will inform (and transform) the way you preach and pastor.

3. **Own Your Work**

   Even though you are not in the marketplace, *you are still a worker*. As a preacher, you have a craft and skill set that you are always laboring over. From time to time, you're unhappy with it, frustrated, and insecure. Sometimes sermon writing feels more like a wrestling match. Like all workers, pastors contend with deadlines and disappointments, successes and failures, office politics, workplace vices and virtues. Preachers *are* workers. The sooner you become attentive to the wonder, heartbreak, and hope of your own daily labors, the sooner you will be able to help others be attentive to theirs. Do you bring your preaching failures and heartaches to the Lord? Do you have preaching confessions and laments to talk with God about? Or do you hold your work back? The sooner you start a dialogue with God about your craft, the sooner you can help others do the same.

4. **Be Teachable**

   Your congregation likely includes plenty of leaders who are more gifted and knowledgeable than you in a variety of sectors and skill sets. Become their student. Perhaps there are senior leaders in your congregation who can teach you something about how to handle conflict, how to manage a budget or a staff, how to lead an organization, how to make a hard decision, or how to develop young leaders. This is not to say that you need to run your church like a business, school, or hospital. Rather, when you honor the wisdom of workers, they notice, and they will receive your sermons differently.

5. **Broaden Your Reading**

   Read articles about what working culture is like outside the church. If you see new essays and opinion pieces about the challenges of remote working, the fears over AI, the downturn in the steel industry, and the rising rates of burnout, don't pass up these articles—read them. Discuss these essays with your workers and allow them to enrich your preaching.

6. **Walk the Markets and Fields**

   Like Paul, inhabit your local marketplace. Walk its sidewalks and patronize local and family-owned businesses. Be a regular at the corner coffee shop or diner. In the Middle Ages, priests were a constant presence in the local markets. They would walk and pray with local farmers around their fields. Pastoral presence matters. But more than that, engaging your local economy will positively inform and locally root your sermons. Great biblical exegesis without a meaningful connection to the local community will fall flat. Carry your markets and the faces of workers with you into the sermon prep.

7. **Keep a Ledger**

   If you're a more data-driven preacher, you might keep a little spreadsheet of your sermon illustrations. How often are you talking about parenting versus work? How often are you talking about relating to neighbors versus coworkers? Sports versus politics, marriage versus markets, white collar versus blue? After six months you can step back and see if your sermon illustrations reflect the expansive mission of God in the world.

Principles for Writing a Sermon on Work

Now you need to sit down and actually write the sermon. Matt Rusten offers preachers four excellent principles for preparing a sermon on work. We offer his principles here in brief and commend his fuller treatment to you in his book *Pastoring for Monday*.

1. Specific over General

As preachers, we love to make lists (e.g., "Live out the gospel as you study, serve, work, and play"). In an effort to be inclusive, we make these lists general and abstract. Generalities are great because no one's left out, no one can complain. Unfortunately, no one's engaged either. While keeping things general is safe, it's not memorable. Lists are inclusive but also dull.

When preaching on calling and career, try your best to be specific. Use grounded examples and down-to-earth stories of very particular workers experiencing very particular challenges. Told in the right way, a narrow story can actually grab a broad audience. Rusten writes, "God seems to have wired our brains in such a way that we can hear specific examples, even about vastly different realities from our own, and translate the message to our own situation; conversely, it can be difficult to hear a general application and make the leap to apply it specifically to our lives."[3]

The preacher's task is to invite a congregation to inhabit a very particular workplace image or story. This story might not include them, and that is okay. Having inhabited this very specific workplace situation, both the preacher and the congregation can work together to explore its broader implications for their diverse callings and careers. In this way, people are no longer the passive recipient of a vague directive to "be more patient wherever you are called." Instead, they are invited not only to inhabit the world of a very specific worker but to imagine the impact of that specific story on their own. Here the preacher includes

---

3. Rusten, *Pastoring for Monday*, forthcoming.

the worker in the task of cocreating a theology of work. The priesthood of all believers is activated through particularity, not generality.

2. Ordinary over Heroic

As preachers, we're often tempted to use larger-than-life stories that are exotic, epic, and heroic. Reaching for exciting images to grab the people's attention, we talk about the *Titanic* or the moon landing, about being a missionary in the distant jungle or a soldier on a far-off battle-field. We talk about global heroes who fight world hunger, racism, or injustice. We quote Martin Luther King or Bono, Churchill or Steve Jobs. While the cosmic scale of these characters and stories might feel attention-grabbing, they can actually be quite counterproductive.

When a person's daily reality is more mundane—busing tables, changing diapers, working the line, and making cold calls—a sermon full of exotic stories of world-changing work will fail to connect. It might even alienate. Preachers should be very cautious when holding up influential activists, celebrities, CEOs, and world leaders as examples. People in your congregation will likely have a difficult time connecting with these world-changing jobs. Matt Rusten argues that "a key question to ponder with any illustration is to ask, 'What level of power or influence does the example assume or require?'"[4] The power of the gospel to transform the small and seemingly mundane should not be overlooked in your sermon. When Jesus wanted to heal the blind man, he did not call lightning down from the sky. He spit in the dirt, made mud, and put it on the man's eyes. There in the dirt, the ordinary was made extraordinary. Seek out sermon illustrations where the miraculous is made known through the mundane. This will help your people do the same in their daily lives.

3. Surprising over Obvious

An investment team has the opportunity to make a lot of money. The new partnership is perfectly legal but it's bad for the world. On the team is a solitary Christian. He has serious reservations about the deal. Will he quit? Will he go along with it? Will he try to torpedo the deal? Will he make a self-righteous speech and storm out?

He does something rather surprising, something unexpected. He calmly tells his team, "I don't think this partnership is in alignment

4. Rusten, *Pastoring for Monday*, forthcoming.

with our team's values. However, if you insist, I will help make this deal happen for you. But I don't want to receive a bonus from this deal. You can keep the profits for yourselves."

Leaders at the Center for Faith and Work in New York would regularly tell some version of this story in introductory classes on the gospel in the workplace. The story was a team favorite because it was rather surprising. There was nothing predictable, cliché, or cute about it. When confronted with a complex workplace situation, the worker did not have a simplistic fight-or-flight response. The story illustrated the surprising and imaginative ways in which the gospel can creatively respond to workplace issues. The daily lives of workers are anything but simple and straightforward. When Jesus transforms workers, he does not turn them into clichés or cartoons. He redeems them to be imaginative and creative in the ways they engage with a complex and broken world.

By grace, this worker demonstrates a redemptive imagination for a difficult situation. Surprising stories like this are invitational. They invite your people to consider how they might transcend the temptations of fight or flight, judgmentalism or capitulation. Through a surprising story, you can activate their imaginations for what it looks like to be a redemptive presence in their own complex callings and careers.

4. Regular over Sporadic

While an isolated sermon or a dedicated sermon series on work can be a wonderful way to jump-start a conversation in your community, the effects of isolated sermons will quickly fade as the topic of work disappears from the pulpit over the coming year. As Rusten notes, "Most preachers understand that congregations are shaped not by particular sermons so much as they are shaped by the consistent, faithful preaching of God's Word. Just as athletes aren't transformed by one workout, our people don't become healthy through one meal."[5]

As opposed to a single Labor Day sermon, we encourage a slow and steady drip of workplace stories and metaphors sprinkled throughout the year. A single sermon will act like a cup of coffee and wake up our waitress, but a sustained and healthy diet of work-oriented sermons will give her the long-lasting energy she needs for a life of faithfulness in the restaurant.

---

5. Rusten, *Pastoring for Monday*, forthcoming.

With this "slow and steady" method, both you and your congregation will slowly become more comfortable and conversant in the deep connections between Scripture and work, labor and liturgy. This slow and gradual pace is your friend. The transformation of people's callings and careers through the power of the gospel is a slow and steady process. Dramatic turns can be unsustainable.

Finally, when preaching about work becomes a regular habit, when it goes beyond the annual Labor Day sermon, *it is at this point* that your people will take you seriously when you tell them, "Your daily work is absolutely central to the mission of this church." This is why Labor Day is not enough.

Resources for Preaching with Workers in Mind

The topic of preaching on work is obviously far too complex to cover in a single chapter. However, if preachers want to grow further in this area, we commend the following resources for their consideration.

Biblical Commentaries
The Theology of Work project offers a free online biblical commentary that is specifically focused on the theme of work. Covering both Old and New Testaments, the commentary examines more than eight hundred passages on the topics of career and calling. This online resource is deep, rich, and dynamic. It was prepared by an international team of theologians, biblical scholars, and marketplace ministry experts. It is free to use at theologyofwork.org.

Books
1. *Faith & Work: Galvanizing Your Church for City Impact* by Lauren Gill and Missy Wallace (Redeemer City to City, 2025) offers practical steps and real-world examples of congregational renewal through the engagement of workers and the marketplace.
2. *Preaching with Cultural Intelligence: Understanding the People Who Hear Our Sermons* by Matthew Kim (Baker Academic, 2017) offers resources for preachers to better connect their sermon texts with the complex stories and identities of their congregations.

3. *Discipleship with Monday in Mind: 16 Churches Connecting Faith and Work* by Luke Bobo and Skye Jethani (Made to Flourish, 2020) offers stories of sixteen congregations that are weaving together faith, work, and whole-life discipleship.

4. *Kingdom Calling: Vocational Stewardship for the Common Good* by Amy Sherman (InterVarsity, 2011) is an imaginative exploration into how your people's diverse callings and careers can contribute to the justice and flourishing of your city and the larger reign of God.

5. *Blue Collar Resistance and the Politics of Jesus: Doing Ministry with Working Class Whites* by Tex Sample (Abingdon, 2006) offers a compelling example of pastoral leadership and preaching that is truly and deeply present with workers—even if you're not doing ministry with "working-class whites."

6. *Sunday's Sermon for Monday's World: Preaching to Shape Daring Witness* by Sally Brown (Eerdmans, 2020) explores the question of how a sermon might help congregants navigate everyday life with the courage and imagination required to testify to the mercy and justice of God.

7. *The Pastor as Minor Poet: Texts and Subtexts in the Ministerial Life* by Craig Barnes (Eerdmans, 2009) guides readers to reimagine the pastor as one who identifies and speaks the life experiences of the congregation through creativity and wonder.

10

Workers Testify

Workers have incredible stories to share.

Throughout their careers, people will experience a wide range of incredible miracles and breakthroughs in the marketplace. Both large and small, these workplace victories fill hearts with joy, energy, and spiritual fire. Deep in their bones, they know, "I did not win this battle; God did." These men and women have good news to share. The church would be wise to listen.

Run and Testify

With feet pounding, sweat dripping, and heart racing, the runner ascends the final hill. He reaches the top, utterly exhausted yet filled with excitement. At the bottom of the hill lies a walled city—his home. Summoning his strength, the runner raises his arms, cups his hands, and shouts his message to the townsfolk below: "WE WON! WE WON! VICTORY!"

Legend has it that in ancient Greece after a tremendous battle against Persia, an Athenian messenger ran a full twenty-six miles back to Athens to announce the good news of victory. The battle had taken place in the small town called Marathon. Two critically important English terms emerge from this episode. The first is obviously *marathon* and the second is *evangelism*.

Euangelion was the Greek declaration of victory; it translates literally as *eu*, meaning "good," and *angelion*, meaning "announcement." When a distant battle had been won, the "evangelist" had the honor of running ahead to proclaim the good news. The city waited in anxious anticipation for the moment when they saw the runner and heard the voice. The evangelist was a storyteller, bearing witness to a distant battle they could not see.

Recognizing the power of this concept, early Christians decided to take it and run with it (so to speak). *Christian* evangelists are those who give testimony to Christ's victory in their lives. Christian evangelists retell the stories of their battles. They testify to the struggle and declare the good news of Christ's miraculous intervention. Panting with excitement, they come before the people and tell the story of what God has done.

Testifying in the Sanctuary

Bearing witness to Christ's victory and testifying to his mighty works have been important threads in the Christian life throughout the ages. Anna Carter Florence, who has studied the historical development of Christian testimonials, argues,

> We can hear [testimony] in Jesus' own preaching and in the witness of the women at the tomb on Easter morning. We can hear it in the apostle Paul's writing and in the *Confessions* of Saint Augustine. The history of Christian communities, from the earliest church martyrs to Puritan membership rituals to contemporary practices of faith sharing, are filled with this ancient Christian pattern for incorporating human experience into proclamation.[1]

The professional clergy have never been able to control or contain the power and urgency of the laity's proclamation. Ever since the women at the tomb proclaimed the resurrection, proclamation and testimony have emerged from unexpected sources. The laity have always found creative ways to share their testimonies of Christ's power in their daily lives. God's people may not be professional storytellers, but that won't stop them. The *euangelion* is too good to be left untold. Even Jesus himself could not stop people from proclaiming him to be the Messiah.

---

1. Anna Carter Florence, *Preaching as Testimony* (Westminster John Knox, 2007), xx.

Why Testimony?

Testimony is what James K. A. Smith calls a "thick practice" in the life of a church.[2] Thick practices are worship elements that contain multiple layers of spiritual meaning and power. They can form a congregation's sense of self and shape their longing for God's reign in their lives.[3]

Too often we have viewed giving one's testimony as a "thin practice," an inspirational story of veiled self-promotion. We inwardly cringe when a church member stands up and begins to tell a story of what God has done in their life. We wonder to ourselves, Is this person testifying to God's greatness or their own?

So, what is the purpose of testimony?

And why should workers publicly tell their stories of victory in worship?

It's true, testimony can be a "thin" practice of self-promotion. When the object of focus is the worker and not the God who was victorious, the story works no good in the congregation. A beautiful testimony is one that points our attention to God, not the messenger. After all, the runner from the battle at Marathon did not run twenty-six miles to talk about himself. His good news was always about the soldiers who actually won the battle.

If the practice of testimony has grown "thin" in your community, here are some thickening agents you might consider.

Recognition: A thick testimony brings the community to a critical point of recognition. Having heard the story, we must acknowledge collectively that this victory—and every victory—belongs to the Lord. A thick testimony begins with the individual contemplating their personal dependence on God, and it ends with the community conceding that communal dependence on God. Thick testimonies name where God has been at work in the life of a believer and encourage the congregation to reckon with God's victories in their own lives. "Yes! God has battled for her. Yes! God is battling for us as well." Testimony invites the community into a state of reckoning. There are battles all around us, and the victories belong to God.

2. James K. A. Smith, *Desiring the Kingdom: Worship, Worldview, and Cultural Formation* (Baker Academic, 2009), 83.

3. The idea of testimony specifically as a "thick practice" came from Sam Hamstra, "The Use of Testimony as a Thick Practice," *Reformed Worship* (blog), August 16, 2018, https://www.reformedworship.org/blog/use-testimony-thick-worship-practice.

Remembering: Thick testimonies also have a memorial function. Being a notoriously forgetful people, the Israelites periodically reminded themselves through the oral practice of sharing, reciting, and storytelling in public assemblies (Exod. 28:29; 30:16; Lev. 24:7; Num. 5:26; 10:9–10; Deut. 16:3). Their memorial practices even took on a physical form with the construction of altars, ebenezers, and memorials built in remembrance. Scripture calls us to cultivate lives of remembrance— take, eat, remember, and believe. The regular practice of storytelling provokes the whole community to remember what God has done, what God is doing, and what God will continue to do in our collective future. A worker's very particular story—well told—can remind a whole congregation of the greater story that God is telling in each one of them.

Recommitment: A thin testimony will be passively consumed and quickly forgotten, but a thick testimony will have consequences for the whole community on Monday. A thick testimony will call people to actively consider and recommit their own work to the Lord. It is not just a sweet story to be heard and then dropped on the floor. When the testimony ends, the congregation responds with an audible "Amen!" which literally means "So let it be!" The people are not passive. The thick testimony activates them to reorient their own stories toward God. Amen, let this story be so among all of us.

Rehearse: Sharing workplace testimonies in the sanctuary is a fantastic way to rehearse sharing your testimony out in the world. If we're called to be a testifying people, we need a place to practice. A thick testimony will invite the whole community to rehearse their own stories of divine victory. In quietly rehearsing their stories in their hearts, they will be better equipped to offer them out loud in the sanctuary and later the world. Sunday's testimony can become Monday's *euangelion*.

The (Im)Possibility of Worker Testimonies

With feet pounding the industrial-grade carpet, sweat staining the oxford, and fingers poised, the worker reaches into his pocket and grabs his phone. Opening LinkedIn, he energetically types his victory announcement. With an uncontrollable glee and a full-faced smile he hits the "Post" button.

A new job secured, a sale finalized, a patient miraculously healed, a college degree completed, a new clinic opened.

Where do workers go with their stories of victory? Where do they go to testify? Some head to the bar to celebrate over a pint. Some take to social media to craft their victory post. Some share it with their spouse over a celebratory dinner. Some, not knowing where to go, run to a quiet stairwell where they pump their fists with vigor. Workers always find a place to tell their stories of good news.

The church, unfortunately, is not one of them. *Your work stories have no place here. Worship is about God, not about you. Stop showing off. Work is hard for everyone. Nobody cares.* Thin church testimonies have unfortunately conditioned people to leave their workplace stories at the door. These workers might have incredible stories to share, but they will never offer them at church.

This is discouraging, but we have good news. While thin testimonies might have discouraged storytelling in your congregation, a few thick ones (well prepared) can invite an incredible wave of unexpected and beautiful stories from God's people.

How to Testify

Tabernacle Community Church in Grand Rapids, Michigan, has made worker testimonies a pillar of their gathered worship time. They have drawn many resources from our partners at Made to Flourish, and their workplace interviews and storytelling practices are shaped by the book *Discipleship with Monday in Mind* by Luke Bobo and Skye Jethani. We hope their leader's guide will pique your curiosity about how you could incorporate something similar in your own community.

All of Life Leader's Guide

We (Tabernacle) believe that "all of life is all for Jesus." In order to demonstrate this reality to our congregation, we added "All of Life Interviews" to our weekly liturgy. During these interviews, we ask three to four questions to various congregants about how they live out their faith in the various parts of God's world. We have a special emphasis on the occupations of congregants because this is where they spend most of their time, but we occasionally have interviews with leaders of ministries within the church or about a congregant's volunteer activities. The interviews typically last for seven to ten minutes and are concluded by having everyone in the congregation who works in a similar field stand up or raise their hands, and then we pray for them as a congregation. We typically do these interviews live on stage but have done some prerecorded as well. The timing is generally something like this:

- One to two minutes: Introduction (Why do we do this? Why is it important? Who are we interviewing?)
- Six to eight minutes: Interview
- Two minutes: Closing Prayer/Commissioning

We try to meet with interviewees two to four weeks before their interview for lunch. We will share a meal, discuss the questions, and provide some coaching on the answers if needed. If possible, we eat near their place of employment and after lunch tour their workplace and meet some coworkers. Finally, we give them the opportunity to meet early on the Sunday of their interview to do a practice run.

Figure 10.1. Worker testimony

Interview Questions

While there can be some customization, these are the four basic questions we ask for the All of Life Interviews. We find that there's value in repeating the same questions each week because of the cumulative effect of hearing these questions on a regular basis.

1. "How would you describe your vocation?" "What will you be doing this time tomorrow?" or "Can you describe a day in the life for you as a _____?"

This question gives us a snapshot into the daily life of the interviewee. It often builds common ground between the interviewee and others within the congregation, even if they don't work in the same field. For example, an engineer and an administrative assistant may have similar tasks as they work to bring order to a chaotic workspace.

2. "As an image bearer of God, how does your work reflect some aspect of God's work?"

The goal of this question is to ground the importance of work in the character and activity of God and to frame our work as an act of "image-bearing." Therefore, we ask the interviewee to directly connect their work to some specific aspect of God's work (creating, restoring, healing, etc.).

Thriving Cities has generated these six helpful categories of God's work that provide a helpful framework:

- the true (the realm of human knowledge and learning)
- the good (the realm of social mores and ethics)
- the beautiful (the realm of aesthetics, design, and the arts)
- the prosperous (the realm of economic life)
- the just and well ordered (the realm of political and civic affairs)
- the sustainable (the realm of natural and physical health)[4]

4. "The Human Ecology: A New Civic Paradigm," Thriving Cities Group, accessed January 31, 2025, https://thrivingcitiesgroup.com/our-framework.

It's easy for people to see the *extrinsic* value of work when it creates opportunities for social interactions, verbal witness, or direct service to people. However, we think it's vital that our congregation sees the *intrinsic* value of their work, the reality that work is good, because God is a good worker and created us to work. We want to show the congregation that work is an opportunity to glorify God by reflecting his image.

3. "How does your work give you a unique vantage point into the brokenness of the world?"

The goal of this question is to give people a dose of reality. We work in a fallen world, and each occupation will have its unique hardships.

This question is important because many people subconsciously believe that their vocation should always be fun and fulfilling, often assuming that the presence of pain and struggle invalidates the goodness of the work. We want to communicate that all work has its struggles and complexities in a broken world.

4. "What spiritual practices have you developed to sustain you in this work?"

The idea behind this question is to get people to dig deeper and think more creatively around what it *looks* like to exercise their faith in their workplace and in a way that influences them and the work they are doing. We try to help prompt people to think deeper without making up a practice.

For example, a lot of believers pray about difficulties at work, but maybe a doctor, nurse, or counselor would take a brief minute before each patient to pray for wisdom and healing. Maybe someone follows a specific routine of praying over their coworkers, customers, or clients on their commute.

Important Things to Remember

1. The congregation is shaped by the cumulative effect of the interviews and the questions themselves rather than the content of any single interview.

2. Diversity is important. If we interview only the people with high-paying, white-collar jobs, it will begin to devalue blue-collar workers. The same goes for age, gender, and types of occupations. It's impossible to

represent everyone in the congregation, but it's very possible to show the congregation a large sampling of jobs, ages, and ethnic backgrounds through the interviews.

3. Be careful of your language. Avoid terms like "full-time ministry" and "sacred/secular" that make church work seem more important than non-church work. Also watch language that positions some work as more valuable than other work (e.g., "We care about all work, from the CEO to the janitor").

4. Meet with the interviewee in person prior to the interview to help them think through the questions, even if you know them well. Don't view this as a waste of time. It's actually a great opportunity for vocational discipleship.

5. Be sure to discuss the dynamics of the stage with the interviewee, such as how to hold the microphone, where to stand, where to look, and how long to speak. It's often helpful to have them rehearse the interview with you.

6. Don't let it become a commercial. It's not a bad thing if an interviewee makes some business connections due to the interview, but that's not the purpose of the interview. Most people are inundated with advertisements and sales pitches, and this will detract from the goals of the interview.

In the space below, write down several people in your own congregation who might be good candidates for a worker interview.

_____

_____

_____

_____

Look at the four questions listed above. How might you need to change or adapt these to fit your context? What might you want to add?

_____

_____

_____

_____

11

Workers Pray

Many photographers focus their work on wide-angle shots of nature, cityscapes, skies, and stars. We look at their massive scale and marvel at their immensity. While it's true that the wide-angle shot can be powerful, consider just for a moment the power of a close-up on a human face. Photographers just love these. Close-ups are real and raw. They're honest. A close-up can reflect back to the viewer something beautiful (and unnerving) about what it means to be human. What it means to be alive.

We might know in our heads that there was a massive earthquake on the other side of the globe. We see a wide-angle shot of a once-thriving city now lying in rubble. We shake our heads and move on. But then a close-up photo flashes across the screen. A woman's face—from that same rubble—and we are drawn in, we are implicated. Through her eyes, we're bound in some mysterious and disruptive way to the human experience of suffering. A satellite image of earthquake damage is something altogether different from a close-up. While a wide angle can induce a sort of compassion fatigue, a close-up can induce a sort of action.

All too often, congregational prayers feel like a satellite image.

Floating high above the ground, these expansive congregational prayers can come off as distant, vague, and detached from the raw honesty of our lives and work down here on the ground. We offer "satellite prayers" for wars to cease, for poverty to end, for cancer to be cured, for our cities to be free of crime and injustice. We pray in broad strokes, sometimes out of necessity and sometimes because we simply do not know how to pray otherwise. The global issues are too large and the answers feel far off. Week after week, satellite prayers can have a way of making our hearts numb and detached.

How can we pray in close-up?
How can we pray while zooming in?
How can we pray with our feet firmly planted on the earth?

Jean is a speech therapist. She works closely with individuals who have suffered from strokes. Sometimes they make progress, oftentimes they have setbacks. Jean describes her work as difficult but rewarding. When she enters into worship on a Sunday morning, she carries her patients with her. Their struggles and prayers become her own. When it is time to pray, Jean makes petitions on behalf of her patients. She comes before God and intercedes for them.

Jean does not pray for all of the world's stroke victims. She prays for hers. She does not pray for all the hospitals in the world. She prays for hers. Jean prays in close-up. She prays with her feet on the ground. How does she do it?

Every week Jean closes her eyes and pictures the faces of her patients. She does this while her pastor prays the following prayer: "May the blessing of God Almighty, the Father, Son, and Holy Spirit, be upon us and through us with all those to whom he sends us, now and forever. Amen." In the stillness, Jean hears God tell her, "Go out and serve *these* people on my behalf."

In ancient Israel, a priest's job was to serve as a mediator between God and a specific community. The priest played an intercessory role. Priests petitioned God on behalf of their particular people and their particular place. Carrying their people and place forward in prayer, Israel's priests would call on the Lord to forgive, uplift, heal, guide, and save the people.

In the New Testament, Christ is our High Priest. In following him, *we all take on a priestly role.* Every follower of Jesus is called to the priestly ministry of prayer and intercession.

Jean, the speech therapist, is leaning into her priestly calling. She has a priestly responsibility to pray for her patients and her clinic. She must intercede on their behalf. She is their priest. Her clinic is her parish. She is not responsible for all patients and all clinics, but she is called to these people and this place.

This is what it looks like to have a close-up approach to prayer.

Satellite prayers are not bad. Sometimes they are very necessary. It is good for congregations to pray about hurricanes, wars, racism, and cancer. It is good to petition God for cosmic levels of healing and restoration. That said, there is something deeply transformative that occurs when God's people learn to pray in close-up.

As pastors and worship leaders, our task is to help our people take on their priestly calling. We must train them to carry before the Lord their *specific* coworkers, their *specific* employers, and their *specific* workspaces. Believing in the priesthood of all believers, we must equip them to petition God directly for the healing, restoration, and renewal of their specific parishes.

As their worship leader, you can begin to train your people for close-up prayers. These prayers will not float passively in the clouds. They will demand an active empathy with the real places and people of daily life. Grab your zoom lens and let's take a look at how you can craft close-up prayers.

Intercessory Introductions

How you introduce your intercessory prayer can have a tremendous impact on how it's experienced. Just a few thoughtful sentences can prepare workers to assume a more intercessory posture. Even in the midst of a satellite prayer, they can be prompted to zoom in and pray close-up.

Examples

- The God of the universe is also God with us. God is not only sovereign, God is radically close. As we come before the Lord in prayer, we lift up the concerns that are closest to us in our homes and workplaces. We offer these concerns and people up before God—their names and faces are on our hearts—and we entrust them to Emmanuel, God with us.

- As we come before God in prayer, we acknowledge that there is so much to pray for that we do not know where to begin. As we pray for God to heal the world, we also ask that he would heal our little worlds.

- As we lift up a few global concerns to God in prayer, let us remember that God is already at work through his people. In millions of small ways, each one of us serves as God's hands and feet, binding up that which is broken in the world. God hears our prayers and invites us to lift up our lives and the lives of those we know and love before him in prayer.

Good introductions can include silence. Invite people to a moment of vocational silence during which they can ponder and visualize their specific petitions, people, and places.

> Picture with me
>> where you will be tomorrow
>> what you will be doing
>>> and whom you will meet.
> And pray with me
>> for the place you will be
>> for the work you've been given to do
>>> and for the people you will serve.[1]

Try writing your own introduction to guide your people into a close-up prayer.

_____

_____

_____

_____

_____

Worker-Led Petitions and Prayers

A good introduction can help workers assume a priestly posture before the intercessory prayer begins. While pastors can lead this time of prayer, sometimes it is advantageous to allow a worker to lead the congregation in prayer.

This might be a stretch for some people who are not comfortable leading in this way, but there is a twofold benefit of worker-led prayers. First, it helps them develop and rehearse a language of prayer and petition. Second, the church has the opportunity to learn with the worker, pray with them, and build a spiritual connection to their sister or brother in the faith that is empathetic and authentic.

1. Written by Uli Chi. Used with permission.

Consider giving the worker a basic template to follow. This not only helps them get started but also can become a familiar format for your congregation's patterns of prayer.

Address: Who God is. Name several divine attributes and actions. Describe God as a worker.

Gratitude: What has God done? What is God doing? For what are you thankful?

Global/National: Name several national or global concerns that pertain to your work or industry. If these are hard to think of, pray for workers globally who do the same work as you but under different circumstances.

  • For example, mining conditions in China and the Congo, policing in Los Angeles and New York, machinist layoffs in Cleveland and Pittsburgh, coffee harvests in Guatemala and Indonesia, engineering projects in Panama and Egypt, software challenges in Seattle and San Francisco.

Community: Name several concerns within your city and surrounding neighborhood and what effect they have on your industry or area of service.

  • For example, a local drought on farming, a housing downturn on construction workers, a new hospital for nurses, a factory closure for machinists, a new shipyard for dockworkers, a new playground for children and stay-at-home parents, a citywide grant for social workers.

Personal: Name a few requests for you, as a worker. Be specific, lifting up your petitions and those of your coworkers.

Amen

If this is difficult to visualize, here is an example of how an auto mechanic might engage this structure.

A Prayer for Auto Mechanics

God, you are the Creator of everything big and small, from the vastness of the cosmos to the intricacy of a small motor. Today, we are grateful for the gift of vehicles. Beyond the comfort and convenience of being able to drive ourselves to places we need to go, vehicles transport needed goods, fresh food, birthday presents, and medical supplies. Thank you for auto mechanics and engineers who can troubleshoot, diagnose, and repair vehicles to keep our society moving smoothly.

Today, we pray for our world. In the midst of conflict, we pray for mechanics who seek to repair vehicles that are needed for safety, for necessary supplies and transport, and for fleeing when necessary. When they lack the parts needed to do so, please provide. We also pray for the devastation of our impact on the globe and the growing threats of global warming. We pray that you make mechanics creative and nimble in their work to create needed energy solutions.

We pray for our country. With the rising cost of supplies and growing inflation rates, many mechanics struggle to keep their work affordable for all. They also are deeply impacted by relationships with other countries on which we are dependent for trading and purchase. As mechanics, make us fair and give us wisdom to navigate the economy well.

We pray for our community. Every day we see and experience first-hand the disparity of wealth and the poverty gap. We improve the expensive import one minute and try to repair the barely functioning car the next. Help us serve all people well, bringing something of your healing and goodness to every client and every vehicle we encounter.

We pray for our church community. We pray specifically for _____.

We also pray that you would make our church community strong and healthy. As the engine is responsible for the smooth running of the whole vehicle, we pray that we, your people, would serve as a healthy engine in your world. We pray that we remain in good repair, that we might leave this place and be agents of healing and stability in your world.

Finally, we pray for the _____ auto shop. We pray for the budget concerns and rising cost of products. We pray for each member of the team—the mechanics who fix, the diagnosticians who analyze, the administrators who deal with details, and the front desk staff who meet customers angry and relieved alike. Hear our prayers for these and for all your auto mechanic children who are called and equipped to serve in this way.

Amen.

This next exercise encourages workers to pray for their own work and the work of others in their same field, considering the shared experience with others around the world.

- Write a short prayer for yourself as a worker.
- Now, think about others who share your line of work. Many of them might be facing unique challenges due to their context or situation. Try to imagine what they might say to God about their work. Try to imagine what God might say back to them. Write a short prayer to God on their behalf. Your prayer will not be perfect; you will make mistakes. That is okay. This is why we call it *practicing* intercession, not perfecting intercession. The very act of standing in between God and a group of people and interceding on their behalf can be a transformative experience. We were made to be priests. Below you can read how one mother not only prays for herself but also learns slowly to pray for all mothers.

God, I pray for my work as a mom. My child has extensive medical needs. There are days that go by where parenting feels routine and uneventful. I thank you for these days because they mean we had no emergencies. This is a gift. There are also days where I collapse in bed in tears, simply grateful we are all alive and have made it through the day. We don't take a single day for granted. I pray for strength to get up and continue care tomorrow. I pray for compassion and patience when I feel frustrated—at insurance companies, schools, my spouse, and sometimes my child. I pray that in your mercy you might heal him and make his body whole—not dependent on life-saving medicine and technology to stay alive. Rest my weary body and quiet my anxious soul as I parent this gift you have given me. Amen.

God, I pray for mothers who have lost a child with the same medical needs as my own because they have been unable to access life-saving medication. Some live in places where there are no pharmacies. Some live in places where pharmacies are under siege and have been destroyed. Some have fled their homes for safety only to be forced to go without what they need to survive. God, I can't imagine the pain, the guilt, the devastation. Would you be close to these mothers in a very real way today? Bring them tangible forms of comfort—friends to journey with them, help where it is useful, and communities that listen and love them in their grief. Work for restoration and shalom in the circumstances around them that have brought them to this place. Rest their weary bodies and quiet their anxious and grieving hearts. Amen.

Creative Prayer Exercise

The theologian Karl Barth once wrote that pastors should preach the gospel with the Bible in one hand and the newspaper in the other. What might it look like to pray in the same way? Take out a newspaper or open a news website of your choice. Grab the top three headlines you see and write them below.

1. _____
2. _____
3. _____

Write a two- or three-sentence "satellite prayer" for each of these headlines.

1. _____
   _____
2. _____
   _____
3. _____
   _____

Now think about a specific worker whose work is impacted by each of these headlines. Write a close-up prayer for these workers.

1. _____
   _____
   _____
   _____
2. _____
   _____
   _____
   _____
3. _____
   _____
   _____
   _____

Get Creative

- If you combine both prayers, you have a paragraph prayer you could use in worship on Sunday. Consider adding the visual element of an actual newspaper clipping on-screen. Cut out the headline and project a photo of it as you pray.
- Think through the workers in your congregation. Coach someone in a similar line of work to write the worker prayer to accompany a headline. They will be able to help the people pray with expertise and empathy.

12

Workers Offer

Do you wish to set up a recurring payment?
  Click here.

With the tap of a finger, your tithe will be digitally transferred every month until the day you die. The work of your hands is offered to the Lord and you don't have to think, move, or feel a thing.

Figure 12.1. Open hands

Long before the COVID-19 pandemic, many churches were shifting their giving to online platforms. The digital method was not only far more convenient for parishioners but also provided a far more predictable and stable flow of income for the church. After all, people pay their mortgages, water bills, and streaming services this way. Why not do the same thing with their tithes and offerings? Funding God's kingdom has never been easier.

But this convenience is not without consequence.

As offering plates gathered dust in the church closet, so did people's understanding of what the offering is actually for. The primary purpose of the biblical offering is not the "funding of the kingdom." Nor is it merely an act of regular obedience. In Scripture, the ritual of offering has a memorial function. It is a time to remember what our world is all about—that our work is connected to and dependent on the larger work of God. Far from convenient or quick, the offerings found in Scripture and the early church were messy, slow, smelly, and wasteful. And as it turns out, there was a good reason for it.

Many of the first Christians did not bring coins into worship. They carried in the actual work of their hands. Like the ancient Israelites before them, their arms were laden with the best fruits from their fields, the fish from their catch, the handcrafted items from their workshops, and the freshly baked goods that came out of their kitchen only moments earlier. These gifts were carried into worship, lifted high in the air, and offered to God as an embodied thanksgiving and grateful praise.

These work offerings were not distant or abstract. Nor were they quick, convenient, or passive. The work offerings were carefully and intentionally gathered and chosen. Then some of the gifts were distributed to the poor, some went to the pastor's family, and finally some of the work offerings were broken open and shared in the Lord's feast. There at the Lord's Table the work of the people was held up as the work of Christ.

You can imagine the odor, the noise, the time, and the production of it all. As the early church grew in size, it increasingly opted for the convenience of currency. After all, coins don't rot or smell, you can transfer them easily, and everyone can use them. It just made sense.

But once again, efficiency has consequences.

Our chosen modes of giving today teach us something important about the ultimate meaning of the offering. Here are some theological truths about the offering that were gradually surrendered and have become all but lost on modern givers.

1. **God truly delights in the unique works of our hands.** Good work that is done well and happily offered emits an aroma that is pleasing to God. God rejoices over businesses that are ethically run, students who are creatively taught, bridges that are sturdily built, and tables that are served with love and hospitality. When these good works are brought

before the Lord with a joyful heart, the Divine Worker is glorified and delighted. Within the context of the digital transfer, it is easy to imagine that God does not care about the quality and beauty of my work; he cares only about the funds provided.

2. **God does not need an offering ritual—we do.** We desperately need a weekly reminder that all our stuff is, quite literally, not ours. We are mere stewards of these families, careers, bodies, and crafts. We are not our own. In this sense, the offering ritual doesn't exist for God; it exists for us. We are possessive and forgetful creatures. God does not need a weekly reminder that everything belongs to him—we do. God is neither hungry nor needy. His kingdom can and will endure without our weekly gifts. God graciously *invites* us to participate in his kingdom through giving, not out of necessity but out of generosity. God will not be changed by what we offer in our worship services—but we might be.

3. **God does not want 10 percent of our income.** God wants our whole selves, our careers and callings, our families and our lives—every piece of us. Notice that the apostle Paul does not ask the Roman Christians to tithe 10 percent. Instead, he says, "In view of God's mercy, . . . offer your bodies as a living sacrifice, holy and pleasing to God—this is your true and proper worship" (Rom. 12:1). Within the context of a digital transfer, it is easy to imagine that the other 90 percent of my money and 100 percent of my life belong to me.

4. **The church is not a charity.** The offering is categorically different from a nonprofit fundraiser. The offering in worship is not a time to make a sales pitch. It is not a time to talk about all the great things the church is doing in the world and all the ways your people need to support it. Nor is it a time to talk about an impoverished child in another country who needs their help. No, a true theology of offering makes the rather audacious claim that it is the wealthy giver in America who stands in need of help and transformation, not the child across the globe. When a congregant places their work on the altar, that worker is freed and healed. It is through the giving that they become rich.

These four truths are part of what makes a rich theology of offering so beautiful and so transformative. Unfortunately, we have lost these riches as we've gradually moved toward modes of giving that are easier and more convenient.

But let's be realistic. Digital giving is not going away anytime soon. It's simply too convenient, practical, and easy. The haunting truth is that bringing back the plates still won't solve our problem anyway. So, in the age of online transfers, the urgent question is no longer "How should we give?" We know how to give. What we've forgotten is how to offer.

How Then Should We Offer?

Your church has all the digital tools it needs to process giving. In the section below, we provide a variety of creative practices for how your people might learn to offer.

Offering Cards

Create an offering card that people can fill out each week and put in the offering plate. Here are a couple of examples you might consider.

Dear God,
  I offer you the service and work of my hands this next week. May these things be pleasing to you;
  [Name several things here. . . .]

I offer all these things to you as my sacrifice of praise and thanksgiving.
  Receive the work of my hands.
  Amen.

Pastor Mike Farley at Central Presbyterian Church in St. Louis provides his congregation with an offering card—with plenty of space for writing a response—that is slightly more holistic.

I offer myself to God in this:
- **Praise/Thanks** (offering gratitude and joy to God)
- **Lament** (offering suffering and pain to God)
- **Petition** (offering requests to God)
- **Commitment to Act** (offering my life to God)

In the space below, write your own offering card to be used by those who give in person and online. Keep it short and simple.

_____

_____

_____

Firstfruits

As you create various methods for offering in your community, consider creative ways to revive the ancient twofold meaning of "firstfruits." You must bring the best and the first from your harvest.

The Best: By the best, you want to encourage people to think through all their various works in the world and carefully select and name the very best things that they would like to offer to God. This involves a sort of childlike posture of pride: "Father, look at this great thing I made!" Here encourage your people to think about something they've done that they're truly proud of, something they might be embarrassed to say out loud. The Israelite farmer would not bring just any animal to God; he would carefully bring the very best.

The First: The first part of the harvest can be an anxious and even nerve-racking time for a farmer. The nearly ripe fruit is vulnerable to destruction. If you give away the first fruits that ripen, you put yourself in a vulnerable position. You have no idea if the rest of the fruit will survive. In giving their firstfruits, Israelite farmers placed themselves in a position of dependence. As you lead offerings for your congregation, prompt them to consider offering something to God from their daily work that is not yet secured or assured. "God of the harvest, this work is not finished, this project is still up in the air, and yet I give it over to you."

Spoken Offertory

Many churches use the offering time for musical gifts. This is a wonderful way to get your members involved and participating, offering up their gifts and talents to God. Amid the music, also allow space for workers, parents, and volunteers to share their brief vocational offerings. An easy way to do this would be to have a short tear-off section in the order of worship that has a one- or two-sentence "offering prayer." Invite people to write their prayer and come to the front and share it while the offering is being collected.

Examples

God, in my work as a <u>professor</u>, I <u>advised new students and received a</u> <u>grant</u> this week. Receive the offering of my hands and use it for your glory. Amen.

God, today I offer you the work of my hands. You equipped me to <u>pour</u> <u>the foundation for someone's new home</u>. In gratitude, I offer this work to you and to my neighbors around me. Amen.

In the space below, write your own fill-in-the-blank offering prompt that you could use in your context.

_____

_____

_____

_____

Get Creative

Bring It to the Altar

- On Labor Day Sunday every year you can do a physical workplace offering. To embody the importance of carrying our work to God and offering it up to him as our thank offering, consider inviting people to bring a work artifact forward during the offering time and lay it down in the front of the sanctuary. Imagine a doctor placing a stethoscope and uttering a short prayer of gratitude and surrender. A shelf stocker at the local grocery store places his apron and box cutter before God, thankful for his part in putting food on tables. A stay-at-home parent places the family calendar or a completed Individualized Education Program for her child on the altar, asking God to meet her in the daily work of her hands. This annual practice would likely take time to develop because it takes our offering one step further from money and one step closer to an ancient Israelite offering of firstfruits. Imagine the beautiful mess of a table in the sanctuary full of workplace artifacts representing the thank offering of our hands.

Children's Artwork Wall

- Similar to the above idea, children can be included in meaningful and formative ways. Consider having an offering "wall" in the sanctuary for children and youth to hang the work of their hands in gratitude to God. They could bring their best artwork or a test for which they studied hard. They could bring a worksheet or watercolor—anything that represents what they did in their work as a student. This is a powerful teaching moment for children of all ages to begin to understand that God delights in their work. They were created to learn and grow, and it brings God joy when they offer up their sacrifice of praise.

  - If you want to take it one step further, have them write a note or a Bible verse on their works of art, then bring them to shut-ins and nursing home members on pastoral care visits. The work of children matters to God and can be used to bless others.

  - Below are some prayers you could use to help children offer up their work to God in a worship service.

Children's Creative Offering

God, in the beginning, you created.
And we are made to be like you.
You are generous to give us all that you created.
And we are made to be like you.
Jesus, you welcome the work of our hands.
And we made it for you![1]

Creator God,
  Bless these gifts and all the work that we, your children, do. We offer it up to you and say thank you. We ask that you bless it and bless our hands, that we might continue to do what you have called us to do. Amen.

---

1. Written by Susan Goforth. Used with permission.

A Surprising "Tithing" Sermon

- Preach an unexpected "tithing" sermon. It is likely that our congregations are accustomed to regularly hearing sermons about the importance of giving: giving to the church, giving to the poor, giving to missions. These sermons often land with the message "Open up your wallets and dig a little deeper. To whom much is given, much is expected." Consider a tithing sermon that has nothing to do with money and everything to do with offering one's work to one's neighbor and to God.

Sung Offertories

- A surprising number of familiar worship songs could be reframed to help people reconnect the work of their hands with their monetary gifts. Consider choosing one that you sing regularly. In between the verses, weave in an offering prayer, helping people recognize that what they are giving is actually themselves. See the example below which applies this technique to the song "Take My Life and Let It Be."
- You can also learn a new offering song and commit to singing it regularly for the next few months so it has a chance to embed itself in your congregation's minds and hearts. Several songs on The Porter's Gate album *Worship for Workers* fit the bill. We've also included at the end of this chapter a new offering hymn text set to the tune of "Blessed Assurance, Jesus Is Mine," written by Hunter Lynch.

Offering Song and Prayer

Here we incorporate stanzas from the hymn "Take My Life and Let It Be."

Gracious God,
  You are the creator, artist, inventor, and giver of all good things. In your wisdom you made this earth and then made us in your own image—to create, invent, work, and give back to you. Today we offer up our lives to you, that you might use us for your glory and the coming of your kingdom.

Take my life and let it be
consecrated, Lord, to thee.
Take my moments and my days;
let them flow in endless praise,
let them flow in endless praise.

Lord, take our hands. We offer them to you, that you might use them
for your good and for your glory. Our hands are often busy. They begin
the day with busy preparations. They type emails and documents that
have the ability to cause ripples of change and progress. They lovingly
bathe a child or successfully prepare a meal. There are very few times
in our days when our hands are idle, so we pray that the works of our
hands would be pleasing in your sight. That our actions would be pure.
That our gestures would cause others to see you. We offer the work of
our hands.

Take my hands and let them move
at the impulse of thy love.
Take my feet and let them be
swift and beautiful for thee,
swift and beautiful for thee.

Lord, take our feet. We offer them to you, that you might use them for
your good and for your glory. Our feet carry us where we need to go.
They can run quickly to someone's aid, they can hastily move away
from someone in need, they can take us in multiple directions leading
down different roads. We pray that our feet lead us down the path of
the cross, where we follow in your footsteps and learn the way of love,
humility, and peace. And as we walk, we pray that others will see you
and also choose to follow. We offer the steps of our feet.

Take my silver and my gold;
not a mite would I withhold.
Take my intellect and use
every power as thou shalt choose,
every power as thou shalt choose.

Lord, take our minds. We offer them up to you, that you might use them for your good and for your glory. Our minds are often so full of information, schedule reminders, to-do lists, and thoughts that need to be sorted out. We have been given minds that are capable of such amazing things, but these minds are also capable of scheming destruction and harm for your earth and for those who dwell in it. By your Spirit, be present in our thoughts and in our hearts. Direct our minds, that in our daily work we might use our intellect to serve you and the world around us. We offer you our minds and our hearts.

*Take my love; my Lord, I pour
at thy feet its treasure store.
Take myself, and I will be
ever, only, all for thee,
ever, only, all for thee.*

Work Be My Praise

Key of C

Text: Hunter Lynch

Music: Phoebe Knapp

♩. = 45

C | F | C | F | C | G

1.Au - thor of la - bor strength - en my hands. Grant per-se -
2.Lord in my wa - ges, make me con - tent. What have I
3.Peo - ple will try me, You made them all. Help me re -
4.You will trans - fig - ure all we have done. When we be -

Ami | D7 | G | F | C

ver - ance through day - light's de - mands. Fill me with fer - vor,
earned that Your hand has - n't sent? I see the li - lies
mem - ber, lest pride - ful I fall. Ev - ery word spo - ken,
hold Him, the ra - di - ant Son Then we will see it:

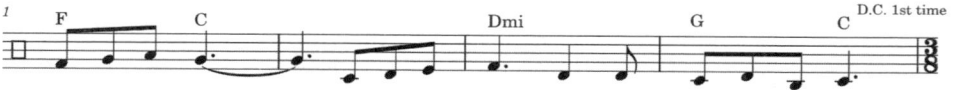

F | C | Dmi | G | C   D.C. 1st time

fire in my bones. May my ways wit - ness to all you have done
here and then gone. Sure - ly my fa - ther won't leave me in want
gui - ded by grace Make me Your ves - sel O Fa - ther, to - day!
(a)har - vest un - moved Un - der a sun where all things are made new

Refrain (alt wording after v4)
G | C | F | C | G | Ami

This is my off - 'ring Hea - ven - ward raised First-fruits up - lift - ed
(our)

D7 | G | F | C | F | C

day af - ter day This is my off - 'ring Hea - ven - ward raised Un - to Thee
(our)

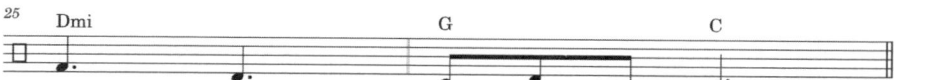

Dmi | G | C

al - ways, Work be my praise
(our)

13

Workers Feast

It was the sixth century and Pope Gregory *himself* was going to be presiding over the local Mass. This was a big deal and the townspeople knew it. They gathered together in reverence and nervous anticipation. As the people processed down the aisle, a woman joined the line and made her way to the front. When it was her turn to kneel, the great pontiff declared that this is "the body of Christ, broken for you." The woman looked down at the bread and cracked a smile. And then—according to some reports—the woman burst out in uncontrollable laughter.

Naturally, this was upsetting to everyone involved. After all, this was *the* pope and he was holding *the* body of Christ. Here—at the most special, most holy moment of Christian worship—a woman was laughing hysterically.

Having calmed down, the woman had to offer some sort of explanation for her outburst. Collecting herself, the woman replied that the loaf of bread resting in the pope's hands was actually *her bread*. She had made it herself, in her little kitchen, with her little oven. Right there in the hands of the pope was the work of her hands.

This is the body of Christ, given for you.

Here at the Lord's Table, the woman experienced a collision of two seemingly very separate realities. Her daily work at her little kitchen table was somehow being connected to the holy work of Christ at *his* table. The connection between her work and his was simply too much to bear.

This beautiful (if somewhat apocryphal) story of Pope Gregory the Great and the woman who laughed is often trotted out for a different purpose. It is commonly used to instruct young Roman Catholics on the doctrine of transubstantiation (bread *becoming* flesh). One version of the story claims that in the face of her laughter and disbelief, God miraculously transformed the bread into a piece of bloody human flesh, thereby shocking and silencing the woman. Be that as it may, transubstantiation is not where we are going to spend the remainder of our time in this chapter.

While academics everywhere debate a *theologian's* question (whether bread can really become flesh), we are more interested in the *woman's* question. It's a question many workers ask: *Can my work really become worship?*

As important as the theological question may be, we are interested in *her* question, *her* wonderment, and *her* struggle to reconcile her daily work in the kitchen with God's work at the altar. How could the "secular" work of my hands become "sacred" worship in his? The laughing woman simply could not put these two things together, and—if we're honest—neither can we.

And yet this is our task, to briefly provide you with some pastoral and practical guides for how you can lead the Lord's Supper in ways that deeply connect with your people's daily lives and work.

Our simple hope is this: As your people look at the bread, they will begin to see new and unexpected collisions between their daily work and his. While we don't expect outbursts of hysterical laughter, we make no promises.

The Divorce Between the Lord's Table and Our Own

All over the world, in every denomination and in every country, workers arrive at the Lord's Table hungry and thirsty. All week long, they've been laboring in an economy that demands more and more. This economy is hungry and thirsty as well. It demands the worker's undivided attention, their complete commitment, their body and soul. Workers spend their weeks playing host at many tables—at restaurants and classrooms, offices and hotels, boardrooms and Zoom rooms. For the sake of others, these workers have poured out all their hosting energy all week long.

Many of these workers feel like the Lord's Table is a million miles away from the tables of their daily labor. They crave a long weekend, a break from the kids, or a round of golf, and the tiny square of bread and the small sip of wine bear little resemblance to the rest and nourishment they seek throughout the week. As pastoral hands break the bread and pour the cup, some may wonder how these spiritual rituals connect to the material rituals of their daily labor. The chasm between the Lord's work and their own opens both wide and deep.

But let's be honest. Reading these words about the separation between the "two tables" might not bother you at all. You might say the tables *should* be distant. The holy sacrament *should* be set apart. The muck and mire of our daily work have no place at the holy table. The work of Christ should be held as different, separate, distinct. The table is the place where human beings leave their work behind and offer their undivided attention to the work of Christ alone.

To this, we have a number of responses. We grant that the gracious work of Christ is—without question—the primary and ultimate focus of the table. It is right and good that we celebrate Christ's sacrifice and his work of grace, not our own. After all, it is Christ's work that ultimately feeds us, and there is no human work on earth that can buy or earn this holy meal.

That said, this is not the whole story of the table.

Let's start with the obvious. Neither the bread, the wine, nor even the table itself dropped out of the sky. Nor did these things just spring up out of the earth. These elements of worship are neither spiritual nor natural—*they are cultural*. Bread, wine, table—such things are the work of human hands. We do not celebrate the feast with raw grapes or whole grains from the earth, nor do we celebrate with mystical elements that magically appeared. No, Christians offer to God the work of their hands—bread and wine require human effort, care, and craft. Turning grain into bread, grapes into wine, and trees into tables requires skill and technology. On the night he was betrayed, Jesus chose to communicate *his* divine work by use of *our* human work. At the very center of their most central act of worship, Christians all over the world engage in a truly strange behavior. *They lift the mundane work of their hands to God and expect that he will use it for something miraculous.*

In the ancient church, the Lord's Supper was directly connected to the liturgy of offering. The people of God would carry in cheese, bread, olives, fish, meat, and wine from their very own kitchens. Some of these offerings would be distributed to the poor, and some would be lifted up and consecrated for the holy feast. There it was—the work of their hands held up as worship before the whole congregation.

Reframing and Deepening Your Table

Below we offer a variety of ideas and resources for your consideration. Our primary hope is not to change your table practices but *to help your existing practices form deeper connections with the lives and labor of your people.* After all, the Lord's Supper is likely one of the most settled and sensitive moments of your worship service. Many churches follow a set form of table practice that has been theologically tested and refined throughout the centuries. For good reason, this is not a moment where pastors have a lot of wiggle room for wild escapades into liturgical creativity. In the examples that follow, we hope to help you take your existing practices and deepen their effect.

There are a number of very simple but powerful ways in which a leader can reframe the table so that workers can better recognize the many intersections between Christ's work at the table and their work in the world. Consider, for a moment, seven very different things a worker might consider as they approach the table:

1. **Workers Examine.** Before they approach the table, congregants can quietly examine their week and confess all the things they have done and left undone. They can ask that their sin-stained hands be cleansed and unburdened before they grasp the bread and the cup.

2. **Workers Thank.** As the works of human hands (the bread and the cup) are raised to God in thanksgiving, worshipers can say a word of thanks for all the ways in which God has been present with them in their daily work.

3. **Workers Approach.** As they approach the table, people can prepare to offer their whole lives at the table to Christ—just as he will soon offer his whole life to them (Rom. 12:1). Perhaps there is something they need to hand over to him at the table.

4. **Workers Receive.** Here workers can open up a tight fist (weary from an economy of grasping and bartering) and, with an open palm of dependence, receive a free gift. In this, they can reckon with God's economy in which nothing can be earned—or lost.

5. **Workers Share.** Congregants can once again behold God's upside-down economy as his gifts are generously shared and distributed to all regardless of education, skill, class, or rank. Here they can ponder their own responsibilities to work and share with generous and open hands.

6. **Workers Hold.** As they hold these two elements that mysteriously intermingle heaven and earth, God and humanity, spirit and flesh, an individual's tidy divisions in their lives between Sunday and Monday, sacred and secular, faith and work can be contested.

7. **Workers Consume.** Finally, as they eat and drink, worshipers can ponder their daily hunger and dependence on Christ. They are not independent titans of industry and success; these workers stand in need of his constant nourishment and presence. Christ can't be their distant Lord on Monday; he must go with them and be in them.

While worshipers will never contemplate all seven of these things in a single trip to the table, these are just a few of the reframings you might offer to your people as they take the bread and the cup. You might consider offering them just one reframing for each meal. If you are interested in learning more about these seven actions, they are discussed in greater theological detail in the book *Work and Worship*.[1]

How to Welcome Workers to the Table

We turn now to offer a series of "table exercises" for workers as they partake in the holy feast. Through these exercises, congregants can gather at the table to (1) remember, (2) participate, and (3) commit to the deep connections between the Lord's work and their own.

Remember

Take and eat, do this in remembrance of me.

When a worker receives this instruction, it is common for them to close their eyes and leave their daily lives behind. In their mind's eye, they are quietly transported to a setting thousands of years ago and thousands of miles away. There they are sitting around the table with the disciples or standing outside the walls of Jerusalem watching Jesus slowly and painfully die for their sins. While remembering the night Jesus was betrayed and the day he died is certainly central to the memorial function of the Supper, we

---

1. Matthew Kaemingk and Cory B. Willson, *Work and Worship: Reconnecting Our Labor and Liturgy* (Baker Academic, 2020).

would like you to consider another memorial provocation that might hit closer to home.

Before your people approach the table, invite them to take a moment to remember a redemptive work that Christ is doing in their own life and work. Think of something broken that Christ has made beautiful. After all, Christ's gracious work did not stop two thousand years ago on a hill outside Jerusalem. He is alive and working today—*at your side*. As you take and eat, do this in remembrance of Christ's work in your life *today*. You work in markets and fields that belong to him.

Remembering can be joyful. It gives individuals an opportunity to reflect on God's goodness and nearness in their daily lives and labor. As they remember, they transition into a state of gratitude. This memorial exercise in the pew prepares their hearts to approach the table with a posture of gratitude. This exercise of remembrance could take a variety of forms:

- Invite silent reflection to remember God's grace in the worker's life and heart. This is followed by an encouragement to come to the table with gladness and joy.
- Invite worshipers to hold a simple stone representing the work of their hands. As they remember how Christ has worked in and through them, have them bring their stone forward and place it on the table before they take the elements.
- Have a few congregants offer a "micro-testimony." Depending on your context, invite a few people to briefly say where they experienced Christ's redemptive work in their week. Intersperse these testimonies with the congregational refrain "We remember, we give thanks." If your congregation is uncomfortable or unpracticed in spontaneous testimonies, solicit these testimonies ahead of time and write and lead a litany of remembrance for them. They will quickly get the hang of it.

But remembering is not always joyful. Inevitably, there will be moments in a worker's week that are painful and cause a high level of discomfort. They remember fudging the numbers slightly to make the report look better. They remember snapping at colleagues and recall their impatience behind the wheel as they rushed to complete their final delivery. Workers remember their weeks not just with gratitude but also with guilt and shame.

Hymn of Remembrance

Remembering with love and hope,
we celebrate the feast.
Christ bids us come and dine with him,
our Host and great High Priest.
Through all our lives, Lord, you are near—
and to the end of time.
In bread and cup yourself you give;
our life in yours we find.

John Paarlberg, "Remembering with Love
and Hope," © 2000. Used with permission.

This guilt and shame might make them hesitant to approach the table. They don't want to approach the feast with dirty hands stained by their work in the world. For those suffering with the burdens of guilt, offer a little time to remember and repent (1 Cor. 11:28). With hands cleansed, a worker can approach the table with a spirit of freedom and joy.

Consider these "table confessions" as a potential starting point:

1. As we prepare to enjoy the gracious work of Christ, we examine our lives and work over this past week. As we remember, we must confess that our hands have grown dirty this week. We have participated in—and even contributed to—sinful patterns and broken systems in our families, our schools, and our city. Looking at our hands, we ask that Christ would cleanse us of all we've done and left undone. We do so with confidence, for the table has been set, the feast has been prepared, and grace abounds.

2. When we gather around the table, we partake in the work of Christ. Before we do that, we confess where our own work this week has fallen short. . . . [Moment of silence]

Many churches use some variation of a "Great Prayer of Thanksgiving." This prayer, like a creed, comprehensively sums up the whole of the Christian faith, offering thanksgiving for all of God's good gifts. It is a prayer of remembering, believing, and giving thanks.

The prayer below is just one example of how to do this. Not every prayer needs to mention work, but look for creative opportunities to celebrate it within a prayer like this.

The Lord be with you.
And also with you.
Lift up your hearts.
We lift them up to the Lord.
Let us give thanks to the Lord our God.
It is right to give our thanks and praise.

It is right for us to praise you, O God, our Creator,
as we lift our hearts and our labors to you.
Through your divine work, you brought forth all that is.
You made ladybugs and lava flows, mountains and mushrooms,
light and dark, and time itself.
You created us, that we might join in your work of creation.
When we were captives, you carved out paths of freedom.
And when we turned away from your love, you went to work—
calling us to remember our purpose and leading us home.
You spoke to us through your servants,
and called us to wait in hope for the day when your creation would
*   be made whole.*

And so, Loving Creator, we praise you
*   and join our voices with all that you have made in the unend-*
*   ing hymn:*

Holy, holy, holy Lord, God of power and might,
heaven and earth are full of your glory. Hosanna in the highest.
Blessed is the one who comes in the name of the Lord. Hosanna
**   in the highest.**

Blessed are you, O God, and blessed is your Son, Jesus Christ,
*   whose calloused hands showed the marks of labor.*
Through his life, Jesus taught us how to serve one another and
*   to serve you,*
*   using our bodies and our talents to build lives of purpose.*

He offered kindness to those who toiled—
in kitchens, in fields, in palaces, in armies.
He blessed the efforts of tax collectors and technicians, stone ma-
sons and sentries.
Through his suffering, death, and resurrection, Jesus overcame
sin and death,
and called us into a new covenant of water and Spirit,
where our labor might be part of the work you are doing in
our midst.

On the night in which he gave himself up for us, he took bread,
gave thanks to you, broke the bread, gave it to his disciples, and
said:
"Take, eat; this is my body which is given for you.
Do this in remembrance of me."

When the supper was over he took the cup,
gave thanks to you, gave it to his disciples, and said:
"Drink from this, all of you; this is my blood of the new covenant,
poured out for you and for many for the forgiveness of sins.
Do this, as often as you drink it, in remembrance of me."

And so, we remember this act, the sacrifice of the workers who
prepared the table which is made meaningful by the ultimate
sacrifice of our Savior, Jesus Christ,
and we offer ourselves to you, proclaiming the mystery of faith:

Christ has died; Christ is risen; Christ will come again.

As we gather this morning, bringing our whole selves to your
holy table
we pray that you might send your Spirit
to fill this bread and this cup,
the fruits of your land and the toil of faithful hands.
Bless our hearts as we receive your Spirit,
and unite us in the light and love of Christ,
that we may serve you and your people with joy and purpose
until you come again to dwell with us
and we sit together at Christ's heavenly table.

Through Jesus the Christ, with your Holy Spirit in the church
that you love,
  we offer you praise and blessing, this day and all days.
Amen.[2]

Participate

The gifts of God for the people of God. Worshipers don't come to the table empty-handed, nor do they come as passive recipients. At the table, people are called to actively participate in the work of God through offering, sharing, and feasting with others. Here are several ideas for encouraging deeper action, agency, and participation.

An Exercise for Working Hands

Consider a worker-focused invitation to the table. "To prepare our hands to receive the work of Christ, I invite you to pray with me using your hands. I will offer you some prompts and lead you through several motions. Please pray with me."

Clenched fists

Clench both of your hands into fists. What were you holding tightly to this week? Perhaps an overscheduled calendar. The pressure of leadership. The expectations you have for yourself and for those around you. The demands of family. Fear. Anger. What are you holding tightly to right now? [Silence] Lord, forgive us. Lord, hear our prayer.

Open palms down

Can you, with the Lord's help, let this thing go? I invite you to slowly open your hands with your palms facing down. Slowly. Slowly. Sometimes that which we hold takes time to even contemplate letting go. As you open your hands, how is God calling you to begin to let go and entrust? Hear God's invitation to trust—to let it go and deposit it into the trustworthy hands that hold it all. [Silence] Lord, hear our prayer.

Open palms up

Slowly turn your hands so that your palms are now facing up. God, we pause to recognize that you have graciously and generously blessed the work of our hands. We offer you our firstfruits from this week—what

2. Written by Calissa Dauterman for the Worship for Workers Project. Used with permission.

we are proud of and what we are grateful for. We offer you our achievements. Our mundane. Our impactful. Through your grace, would you transform our ordinary work into something extraordinary? Include these hands, we pray, in work that serves your kingdom and glorifies your name. [Silence] Lord, hear our prayer.

Outstretched hands

I invite you now to reach out and extend your hands to the window and the city outside. They are still your hands. But in this gesture move them away from yourself and toward the world outside. God, what might you place in our hands? God, how might you use our hands? What gifts are you giving? What work are you preparing? What will you place in these hands that are now cleansed and open? [Silence] Lord, hear our prayer.

We offer you these hands, trusting that you will bless and direct them tomorrow and always. Feed us, nourish us, use us, and send us. Amen.[3]

> God, we bring you the work of our hands now
> Lay it down, lay it at your feet
> What we've done, what we've built, what we've broken
> Lay it down, lay it at your feet
>
> You hold it all, Jesus
> You hold it all
>
> Worried hearts, wearied hands, weakened bodies
> Lay it down, lay it at your feet
> What we've used, what we've lost, what we've wasted
> Lay it down, lay it at your feet
>
> All our dreams, all our plans, our ambitions
> Lay them down, lay them at your feet
> And even if nothing comes to fruition
> Lay it down, lay it at your feet
>
> —"You Hold It All" by The Porter's Gate

3. This is a vocationally conversant adaptation of a similar working hands prayer led in a retreat by Chris Schoon. Its beauty lies in the fact that it has undergone multiple adaptations for different contextual moments. Continue to adapt and use these embodied motions to help your congregation pray. Original source of the prayer is unknown.

In an individualistic economy that encourages self-promotion and self-enrichment, the table offers workers a more communal alternative. It has its own economy as a place in which the work of our hands exists not for the sake of self-enrichment but for the nourishment and flourishing of others. Hands are not grasping and trading with anxiety at this table. With joy and freedom they're giving and receiving. At the Lord's Table, we're not individual consumers; we're a body, a community. Constance Cherry reminds us that the very word *communion* indicates the "blessing of the community's oneness in Jesus Christ. It is a time for celebration, and a reflective appreciation for the mysterious way in which God binds us together in holy fellowship."[4] Employed or unemployed, blue collar or white, or no collar at all—all are welcome in this economy. All receive freely, and no one leaves hungry.

An Exercise for Participation in the Table Economy

How might you creatively teach the communal nature of this table economy? How might you illustrate the upside-down nature of commerce at the table? Here are a few ideas to get you started:

- If you have flexibility in your space, celebrate communion in a way that invites your people to actually look at one another as they partake. Whether they stand in a large circle or make eye contact with others as they walk up and down the aisle, remind people that they do not celebrate this feast alone. You may, for example, have them turn toward each other and speak a word of encouragement or blessing to one another. Finding small ways to undermine spiritual individualism at the feast is important. Your call is to have them behold the larger body—the broader economy of sharing and grace—of which they are a part.

- Early in the service, offer a congregational prayer of confession that names the ways our nation, cities, and workplaces are spaces of division and disunity. As they come to the table, offer a prayer that builds a conceptual bridge between that experience of disunity and enmity in the world and the peace and reconciliation we can experience at the table. Consider the following words as a starting point on which you might build.

> *Prince of Peace, we confess that we are not peaceful. Our nation and our city, our workplaces and our families are spaces of*

4. Constance Cherry, *The Worship Architect* (Baker Academic, 2010), 88.

division and disunity. As we prepare to gather around your table
of peace and reconciliation, convict us of the ways in which
we have widened those divisions, the ways we have sought
our victory over your peace. As you make your peace with us
at this table, make us into ambassadors of your peace in our
city. Amen.

- You can offer the following prayer that emphasizes the strange and rather upside-down economy of the table. It rather provocatively illustrates the difference between the gracious exchanges that happen at this table and the sometimes grasping exchanges that can happen in the world. Please note that a prayer like this might be disruptive in your congregation. However, framed wisely and pastorally, liturgical disruption is not always a bad thing.

What do you bring to Christ's table?
We bring bread,
made by many people's work
from an unjust world
where some have plenty
and most go hungry.

At this table, all are fed
and no one turned away.
Thanks be to God

What do you bring to Christ's table?
We bring wine,
made by many people's work
from an unjust world
where some have leisure
and most struggle to survive

At this table, all share the cup
of pain and celebration
and no one is denied.
Thanks be to God

These gifts shall be for us
the body and blood of Christ,

our witness against hunger,
our cry against injustice,
And our hope for a world
where God is fully known
And every child is fed.
Thanks be to God[5]

Commit

This is how you are to eat it: with your cloak tucked into your belt, your sandals on your feet and your staff in your hand. Eat it in haste; it is the LORD's Passover.

—Exodus 12:11

We cannot recline at the feast forever; we are called to go, and there is much to do. The table is set for people who need to get moving. This table has consequences. It has purchased us for mission. Roman Catholics communicate the missional reality of the table with the declaration "*Ite missa est,*" which means "Go, it is sent."

For the ancient Israelites, the belt, sandals, and staff communicated something very important about the mobile and active nature of the Passover. The belt was a symbol of preparedness for activity and action. The sandals symbolized their public life out in the wilderness and the larger world. And the staff symbolized the length of the journey that lay ahead. While it's difficult to find a good staff these days, we would like to encourage you to think about how you will communicate the *missional* nature of the table.

This table points us to a new way of living and working in the world. In the next chapter, we will discuss how to bless and send workers back into the city. But a short bridge prayer between the end of communion and the end of the worship service can help a worshiper make sense of what has just happened and why it matters for their work tomorrow.

We know that the table commits us to a certain pattern of life and work. But how do we communicate this to our people? A closing table prayer with the following structure can help.

5. "To Christ's Table We Bring Bread Made by Work in an Unjust World Where Many Go Hungry," Theology of Work Project, accessed April 22, 2025, https://www.theologyofwork.org /book/work-in-worship/prayer-material-for-services/offertory/to-christs-table-we-bring-bread -made-by-work-in-an-unjust-world-where-many. Used with permission.

1. Address to God
2. Thanksgiving for the work of the table
3. Prayer of commitment for our work in the world

Example 1
Bread of Life,

You have gathered and nourished us with your body and blood. Thank you for the gift of our salvation and for the grace you have so freely given. Thank you for tangible reminders of your love for us through these gifts of bread and wine.

With these gifts, may we go now into whatever this week may hold, offering up our gratitude, thanksgiving, and the work of our hands. Amen.

Example 2
Lord God,
in deep gratitude
for this moment, this meal, these people,
we give ourselves to you.

Take us out to live as changed people
because we have shared the living bread
and cannot remain the same.

Ask much of us, expect much from us,
enable much by us, encourage many through us.

So, Lord, may we live and work to your glory,
both as inhabitants of earth
and citizens of the commonwealth of heaven. Amen.[6]

With these examples in hand, try writing your own prayer that connects the work of the table to your people's work in the world.

Address: _____

6. Iona Community, "Concluding Prayer from Liturgy of Holy Communion A," in *A Wee Worship Book*, quoted in Emily Brink and John Witvliet, eds., *The Worship Sourcebook*, 2nd ed. (Baker Books, 2013), 351–52.

Thanksgiving: _____

_____

_____

_____

_____

Commitment: _____

_____

_____

_____

_____

14

Workers Scatter

Last Words Matter

> Thanks for coming. It was great to have you all here with us. Have a great week and we'll see you for worship next Sunday!

You've already lost them. Parents are whispering to each other about which one is responsible for the nursery pick up. Someone is pulling out a cell phone to check on the big game. The musician is minutes from pulling the plug and wrapping cables. The hospitality team has already left the sanctuary to head to the fellowship hall. People are already checking out of worship. And if you're honest, there might be weeks when you checked out as well.

All your creative energy went into planning the earlier parts of worship and you didn't really think about how you wanted to end it. *Closing with one extra chorus will suffice. Let's keep it easy*: "Thanks for coming. See you next week."

While often ignored, the last few minutes of worship are absolutely critical for your people. Like the opening welcome, the final dismissal frames everything we've done in the sanctuary and everything we're about to do in the world. The final words are not just the necessary filler to get people out the door. Closing words help worshipers make a critical connection between what they have just done in the sanctuary and its consequence for what they are about to do tomorrow.

Worship is not over. This is the launching pad for a whole week of worship. Our "time with Jesus" is not over. He goes beside and before us into the city, our homes, and our work. We will meet and serve him there. Whether you call it the dismissal or the benediction, the last two minutes are absolutely critical. Our gathered worship in the sanctuary must now become our scattered worship in the world.

A good sending always includes two things: a blessing and a charge.[1] First, workers must receive words of blessing. "May the Lord bless you and keep you." These beautiful words remind your people that they never face the work alone. They must never be told, "Go and serve the Lord!" without the promise and the comfort that the Lord goes with them. Just as Jesus has been present with them in their worship, he promises to be with them in whatever their week might hold. These words of blessing should echo in the worker's ears as they walk into the restaurant, the boardroom, and the classroom. When they face an angry customer or clean up yet another round of dirty dishes, Jesus is with them—beside them, above them, beneath them. They are never alone.

Second, workers must receive a charge: "Go out into God's world to love and serve." They receive this charge because—as it turns out—God's blessings have consequences. Christ has forgiven, redeemed, and blessed you *for a bigger purpose, a larger plan*. The ultimate purpose of this worship service is not to comfort *you*, teach *you*, or feed *you*. The ultimate purpose is that you would go out into the city to comfort, teach, and feed *others*. As Christ has done a great work in you, now you must leave and live out that gracious work in the city.

Don't be afraid of giving your people a charge. The charge honors them. Their work has urgency, meaning, and purpose. God has called them to serve and has equipped them well. And now God sends them out.

The blessing and the charge are profoundly interdependent. Think for a moment about what happens when people receive one without the other.

---

1. This two-part framework is laid out and well detailed by Constance Cherry in her book *The Worship Architect: A Blueprint for Designing Culturally Relevant and Biblically Faithful Services* (Baker Academic, 2021). Our handling of this material is dedicated to crafting vocationally conversant sendings. For a deeper biblical and theological understanding of sending, we encourage you to read her work.

Without a blessing, a pastoral charge can be crushing for a worker. As the pastor, you have no idea what challenges your people are facing Monday morning, but they certainly do. Some of them feel trapped at work, broken down and utterly alone. When the pastor shouts "Charge! You can do it! Go and serve the Lord!" these words are received as an impossible burden of responsibility. Giving workers a charge without a blessing is a spiritually isolating, empty, and burdensome experience. Your people must receive an assurance that they are not alone, that everything is not up to them.

A blessing without a charge can also be destructive. Its destructive power, while equally nefarious, comes in a much slower and more subtle manner. Without a charge, the final blessing teaches workers to see the sanctuary as a place where they "get blessed." This is a place of comfort and self-affirmation, a place where God's blessings can be freely imbibed with no public obligations or consequences. A blessing without a charge has no forward momentum, no weight, no urgency propelling people into the city. When workers experience aimless blessings week after week, they settle into lethargic comfort—a state of grace that demands nothing of their gifts, talents, and realms of responsibility. They also must return to keep getting more. God's blessings stop at the sanctuary door.

Regardless of your worship style, your people need both a charge *and* a blessing. The task of the last two minutes of your service is to reorient workers toward the mission of God in the community with the assurance of God's presence and power that go with them.

As an initial exercise, consider the sending words we quoted at the beginning of this chapter. Consider the consequences of these words and how a simple rewrite could have completely transformed their impact.

Rewrite

What a gift to worship together today. As we go from this place, our worship now continues in our daily living. So go now into God's world to serve others with your whole heart and your whole self. And know that you go with God's blessing and promise—you are never alone. May the Lord bless you and keep you as you serve. Go in peace.

In the space provided, practice a few rewrites that might work in your own context.

Sample: We're so glad you came. Come back again next week. Don't forget we have potluck!

Rewrite: _____

_____

_____

Sample: It was wonderful to worship God together. Keep doing it this week.

Rewrite: _____

_____

_____

Sending Songs

If our final words matter, the same is true for our final song. We did a quick survey of several hymnals to determine how many songs were labeled "closing songs." The numbers confirmed what we suspected. Less than 1 percent of songs in printed hymnals from several denominational backgrounds were closing songs. We have an abundance of opening songs, praise songs, prayers, and laments. But our options for service closers are so few that we are forced to improvise and make do. Here we can't help but note our disappointment with the term *closing songs*. Our time of weekly worship is not "closing." Indeed, it is only just beginning! This is why we've chosen the term *sending songs*.

Finally, given the relative paucity of final songs, we've partnered with the songwriting collective The Porter's Gate to commission a whole album of sending songs. This album has many new songs that are congregationally singable and will send your people with both a blessing and a charge. With that noted, please consider the following exercise.

List your three or four most sung closing songs:

1. _____
2. _____
3. _____
4. _____

There's a possibility one of the songs in your closing repertoire is either the Gloria Patri or the Doxology. Both are beautiful, trinitarian songs of praise with formational value for worshipers. But neither do the work of sending or charge.

It's also possible one of the songs you listed offers your people the promise of escaping the world one day and going to heaven. While a vision of the heavenly city is indeed comforting, you are about to send them into *your city*. The verses below are quite beautiful and rightly loved; however, their lyrics don't send people out with a sense of purpose.

> O Lord, haste the day when my faith shall be sight,
> the clouds be rolled back as a scroll;
> the trump shall resound and the Lord shall descend;
> even so, it is well with my soul.
>>   —"It Is Well with My Soul" (v. 4)

> Turn your eyes upon Jesus,
> Look full in his wonderful face,
> And the things of earth will grow strangely dim,
> In the light of his glory and grace.
>>   —"Turn Your Eyes upon Jesus" (v. 1)

> Finish, then, thy new creation. Pure and spotless let us be.
> Let us see thy great salvation perfectly restored in thee.
> Changed from glory into glory, till in heaven we take our place,
> Till we cast our crowns before thee, lost in wonder, love, and praise.
>>   —"Love Divine, All Loves Excelling" (v. 4)

What do these songs (beloved as they are) communicate to workers about where they are being sent?

_____

_____

_____

_____

For the three songs you listed above from your own congregation, consider if they do the work of charge, blessing, both, or neither. Do they name our responsibility to go into the world to love, to serve, and to seek justice and mercy?

1. _____
_____
_____

2. _____
_____
_____

3. _____
_____
_____

How might you take what you already sing and make it more complete? Write a one- or two-sentence framing (a short verbal introduction or conclusion) before or after your three songs. Add blessings and charges as needed.

1. _____
_____
_____

2. _____
_____
_____

3. _____
_____
_____

Example

God sends us out this week into our daily work as those who are called to bring forth the kingdom and live as members of the new creation. This gives meaning to our lives and hope for our callings. Go now, with the promise of God's presence that will fill you with wonder, love, and praise.

> Finish, then, thy new creation. Pure and spotless let us be.
> Let us see thy great salvation perfectly restored in thee.
> Changed from glory into glory, till in heaven we take our place,
> Till we cast our crowns before thee, lost in wonder, love, and praise.
> —"Love Divine, All Loves Excelling" (v. 4)

Sample Scatterings

Sample 1

Go into the world:
Dance, laugh, sing, and create.
We go with the assurance of God's blessing.
Go into the world:
Risk, explore, discover, and love.
We go with the assurance of God's grace.
Go into the world:
Believe, hope, struggle, and remember.
We go with the assurance of God's love.
Thanks be to God.[2]

Sample 2

Friends, this is not the end of our worship but its beginning.
We go now into the city to continue lives of worship and service:
In the marketplace and the storeroom,
In the medical facility and the classroom,
In the quietness of retirement and the hustle of household.
And so we go, to extend our worship into the world.
We go, to extend these songs of grace and mercy to our coworkers and classmates.
We go, to extend this table of hospitality to our neighbors and family members.
We go, trusting that God is at work in this world, using us and our gifts for his glory.
We go, equipped with the power and presence of the Spirit, who goes out before us and lights our path so that we might love and serve.
Amen.

Sample 3

We have assembled together in this place as the gathered body of Christ, lifting our voices to proclaim Christ to the world through our worship.

2. Emily Brink and John Witvliet, eds., *The Worship Sourcebook*, 2nd ed. (Baker Books, 2013), 360. Used with permission.

**We prepare to leave now as the scattered body of Christ, lifting
our voices, for Christ is with us in our work in the world.**

As lab techs and lawyers, as firefighters and farmers,
Christ is with us in our work in the world.

As tellers and teachers, as accountants and auto mechanics,
Christ is with us in our work in the world.

As managers and marketers, as nurses and nannies,
Christ is with us in our work in the world.

As engineers and event planners, as postal workers and
production managers,
Christ is with us in our work in the world.

As salespeople and social workers, as cashiers and construction
workers,
Christ is with us in our work in the world.

As you go, know that you do not go alone.
Your work is held in the power and covered in the blessing of
the triune God.
May the love of God the Father, the grace of the Lord Jesus
Christ,
and the fellowship of the Holy Spirit rest, rule, and abide with
you all
as you carry Christ in your work in the world. Amen.[3]

Conclusion

Congratulations! You made it through the heart and soul of this handbook.
We hope that your imagination is fueled with possibilities for your unique
context.

We are now going to pivot our attention. While this first section focused
on workers and how they experience worship, the final sections focus more
directly on you as a leader of worship.

You are a worker as well. You have a unique set of victories, burdens, and
longings in your own daily work. You, too, need to carry your work before

3. Written by Anthony Bolkema. Used with permission.

the Lord. Our deep hope is that you have not only the resources you need but also a renewed sense of calling to do the beautiful (and sometimes challenging) labor that God has set before you. We thought it appropriate to bless you and send *you* before we move on.

Dear friends, called to the labor of leading worship,
Hear and receive this blessing.

God go before you to lead you
Behind you to protect you
Beneath you to support you
Above you to watch over you

God go beside you to befriend you
Do not be afraid
May the blessing of the Father and Son and Holy Spirit be on you
—"Reformation Blessing" by The Porter's Gate

PART 3

HOW TO BLESS WORKERS' CALLINGS

15

Blessing Callings and Careers

Imagine if your church were to offer a Sunday school class on the topic of faith, work, and the Bible. Imagine further if a group of workers in the construction industry were to attend your particular class. For eight straight Sundays, these plumbers, electricians, framers, engineers, and real estate agents would all walk into your church to attend your class. There, depending on your skills as a teacher, these workers would sit and learn from you about the important place of work in Scripture and the general mission of God.

A moment of truth: On its own, the lasting impact of your Sunday school class will be limited. Construction workers will struggle to connect your general theological concepts about work to the very specific and very complicated challenges and issues they face in their industry. They will likely forget many of the theological terms and ideas you offered them. To make matters worse, they will have to work out the details of living these concepts on a day-to-day basis all by themselves. After all, how much do *you* have to teach these workers about the construction industry? How much do *you* know about the life of an electrician, a plumber, or a real estate broker? Sure, you might have some general ideas, but ultimately, these workers will need to figure things out on their own.

Now imagine a second scenario. Instead of teaching these workers how to follow Jesus in the construction industry, *you try to learn from them*. Imagine that you invite them to join you for lunch and conversation. Perhaps you join them at a construction site or in an engineering firm. Once everyone is seated, you ask them a series of questions about their daily struggles and joys in the industry. You ask them what they hate and what they love and long for in their daily work. What are the stereotypes about engineers and electricians? What are the unique virtues and vices for folks on the job site? What's beautiful and what's broken? Imagine you take notes on what they teach you.

After your meeting, you go home and take thirty minutes to write prayers for workers in the construction industry based on what you've heard. On Sunday morning, you invite these workers to come forward and you ask members of the church to surround them and lay hands on them as you pray the prayers you've written just for them. Do you think that these plumbers, framers, and real estate agents will soon forget this moment? A few minutes on a Sunday morning and you've imprinted on these workers a lifelong memory and a vision for their unique calling in the industry.

Sure, your basement Sunday school class might have some genuine intellectual impact on how these workers think about the place of work in Scripture, but this congregational prayer is something different. *Teaching about work in the church basement is somehow different from praying for workers in the sanctuary.* The hands, the surrounding congregation, the vocational specificity, the naming of building sites, safety issues, and housing markets—it all combines to mean something different, something more. You know intuitively that there is a difference between Sunday school and the Sunday prayer. You can feel it. But why?

There are at least five major reasons for the difference:

1. Sticking workers down in the basement and inviting them up to the front communicates two very different things about the place, the importance, and the urgency of their unique contributions to the kingdom of God.

2. Your lunchtime questions invited (forced?) these workers to do the theological and spiritual work for themselves. They had to spiritually examine the construction site in a way some of them might never have done. Rather than being passive listeners to a theological expert, the workers had to wrestle with the unique spiritual joys, struggles, temptations, and contributions of their particular industry. They had to *do theology* themselves.

3. Through your questions, you demonstrated to them that you are a pastoral leader who is genuinely curious and teachable. In positioning

yourself as a learner—rather than a teacher—you built a bond with these workers that you did not have before.

4. You engaged their bodies. The physicality of standing up, coming forward, and being visible before the whole congregation had an impact on them. Surrounding them with the bodies and hands of the community meant something as well.

5. All of this culminated in the unique specificity of your prayer for the construction industry. It wasn't perfect. You may have even gotten some of the details wrong. *But that does not matter.* Your prayer brought the construction industry right to the center of the whole congregation. Their unique joys and day-to-day struggles were the center of attention. They were named in God's house and—for a few special moments—all God's people stood in solidarity with these construction workers and prayed on their behalf. They were neither alone nor anonymous. Their God, their pastor, and their community saw them and stood with them.

Remember Who You Serve

These ceremonies of vocational blessing can help your workers remember who they are, why they work, and who they serve. Being forgetful, human beings are prone to lose sight of their answers to these central questions. Vocational blessings like these can play a crucial memorial function in your community's life.

The people of Israel were notoriously forgetful. They constantly forgot God, his commands, his promises, and his covenantal love. The Israelites were constantly forgetting their history of hard labor in Egypt and how God had heard their cries and saved them. Wandering in the desert, they started to imagine that maybe working for Pharaoh wasn't so bad. Laboring in Canaan, the Israelites quickly forgot that the land, water, and harvest were all from God. In response to the forgetfulness of Israel's workers, God did more than set up a theology class about work; God gave the Israelites worship, sacrifices, rituals, prayers, and feasts for the purpose of remembrance. Worship has always had a powerful memorial function.

In this chapter, we will help you develop your own tradition of blessing various callings and careers within your congregation. We will explore how to schedule these blessings, how to prepare and structure them, who to include, and more.

The instructions that follow are designed to be malleable to your particular context. They can function like an accordion—you can expand or contract them depending on the amount of "stage time" you wish to dedicate to them. You can also adjust our examples to fit your vocational context (more agricultural vs. commercial, urban vs. rural). Also, remember that we are blessing *callings* and not simply *careers*. You should be careful to make space for the blessing of students, parents, the retired, volunteers, and others who are not paid but labor all the same.

A Prayer for Customer Service Representatives

Today we pray especially for those who serve as customer service professionals.

God, we celebrate that they have the opportunity to model Christ to others by being a servant to those in need. We thank you that they can have friendships with coworkers and know they are not alone in the task you have given them.

We lament with them that though they are tasked with providing great customer service, there can be conflicting expectations from their customers and their management—causing confusion, frustration, and exhaustion.

We repent for the ways customer service jobs are often overworked and overlooked. As your people, may we learn to be people of gratefulness and gentleness toward those who are working these frontline jobs. Help business owners and managers to provide workplaces that meet the needs of their employees, so that as they serve, they can thrive.

We ask, O Lord, that those in the customer service industry might be given divine patience as they seek to serve people. May they see each person they serve as an image bearer of God.

May the fruit of their labor be used for your kingdom here on earth. May the Spirit's fruit in them be a light to all they come in contact with. May the skills they develop be used in your church and for your glory. Amen.

Written by Travis Jamieson. Used with permission.

How to Frame a Specific Calling

Before you bless a specific calling or group of workers, you will need to teach the congregation a bit about the calling or career itself. Be they mothers or medical professionals, students or software engineers, you are going to have to introduce what it's like to work in this field—its raw reality, its specificity, its beauty, and its brokenness. It needs to be quick, clear, and effective. In order to understand who these workers are and what they are going through, the congregation is going to need some sort of framework. Of course, you can do this yourself by doing your homework, taking time to learn about the field by interviewing workers beforehand. Another option is to invite a worker or a group of workers to come up front and speak for themselves. Workers can prepare brief testimonies or take part in an interview in front of the congregation.

Whoever is speaking, they will need some sort of framework for introducing the congregation to the specific job in question. We have found the threefold biblical structure of creation, fall, and redemption to be a particularly easy and effective way to quickly frame any industry or field. Every worker experiences some sort of creational wonder and joy at work (creation); they all experience some sort of heartbreak, temptation, and frustration (fall); and they all see and long for some sort of transformation and hope (redemption). The leader's task is to help the congregation see the unique goodness, brokenness, and healing that can be found in this particular line of work.

In the creation section of the framing, you are looking to isolate and illustrate the inherent goodness, value, and fun of the job or field—its wonder and joy.

- What does creativity, value, and positivity look like here?
- How is God the Creator glorified by our craftsmanship, care, and stewardship in this calling?
- How does this industry or calling contribute to the flourishing of the broader community?
- Why do we need it?

In the fall section, you are looking to frame the unique trials and tribulations of work in this field or vocation—its heartbreaks and temptations.

- What does injustice look like here?
- What are the vices and stumbling blocks that you face?
- What makes it hard? What makes you cry?

In the redemption section, you are trying to frame the unique ways in which Christ's victory, healing, and love are active in this particular industry or calling—its transformation and hope.

- How is Jesus challenging and even changing you in and through this work?
- How is he changing your heart?
- How is he calling you forward into a new future in his present and coming kingdom in and through this work?

This threefold framework helps the whole congregation avoid either demonizing the job as worldly or romanticizing the job as flawless. Framed within the work of Christ's redemption, the congregation cannot dismiss the job as mundane, meaningless, or merely secular. Understanding all our callings within the framework of creation, fall, and redemption places our particular work squarely within the scope of the gospel and the mission of God. We will use the example of restaurant workers to illustrate.

Creation
- Here you might name the goodness and beauty of food, flavors, and communal feasting. You might name the value and importance of a well-cooked and well-served meal, of hospitality and conviviality, the ways in which restaurants can be places of fun and friendship, celebration and family. Your task here is to name all the ways in which restaurants contribute to what makes for a great town or city.

Fall
- Here you might name the ways in which workers are struggling in the restaurant industry: low pay, job insecurity, long hours, sore feet, and widespread struggles with exhaustion, alcoholism, and depression. Perhaps the workers have told you about their struggles with difficult customers or their frustrations with tipping culture. You can name

and report on the troubles and tears that the waiters and waitresses named for you.

Redemption

- Here you might give thanks for and pray for Christ's transformative presence with these workers as they engage the restaurant industry. You could lean on Christ's priestly calling to be a healing and reconciling presence in the restaurant, his royal calling to be good and responsible stewards of our gifts, and his prophetic calling to tell the hard truth about the pain and injustice that is going on in the restaurant industry. In Christ, your prayer is that he would make them salt, light, and yeast in the city's restaurants.

A Charge or Vow

Having framed the workers' experience and their important place within the larger work of God and your community, you might now consider commissioning the workers by offering them a specific charge or a series of vows that they might affirm before the congregation. Of course, this is optional, and you might decide—for a variety of good reasons—to forgo this option. After all, the language of "vows" and "charges" might feel overly serious, authoritarian, or even legalistic to you.

Nevertheless, you might consider vows and charges for a couple of reasons. First, a series of vows will not necessarily feel demeaning to the workers at all. Vows actually honor the urgency and value of their work. After all, the community would suffer if they did not do their job well. Moreover, followers of Jesus should build, sell, police, teach, litigate, and parent in ways that truly honor their Lord and Savior. Taking a solemn vow to work in these fields in a way that glorifies God honors the kingdom importance of their daily labors. We make vows to our God, our spouse, and even our country because these things matter—they're important. The same is true for our work.

Second, you should consider public charges and commissions because prayers and blessings in the sanctuary have public consequences. Workers need to publicly respond to your blessing by being a blessing to others out in the streets. We must learn to say, "May God richly bless your work in this city's courtrooms so that you can be a blessing to others. May God give you the legal arguments and skills you need so that you might pursue the cause of justice and the glory of God—not your own."

If you decide to move forward with giving a charge or a series of vows, it goes without saying that you need to have a preliminary conversation with the workers. Your vows should emerge from listening carefully to them. Where are they tempted, where do they stumble, what do they need to remember, and what should love of neighbor (and enemy) look like in their particular industry?

How to Schedule

There are a variety of ways to schedule these blessings. One option is to select one vocation per month. You can be as general or specific as you like. General categories might include medicine, hospitality, business, technology, education, finance, first responders, mothers, fathers, students, and the retired. If a surly congregation member complains, "You have not blessed my vocation yet!" you can simply reply that their month is coming soon and you would appreciate their help in organizing it. After all, the months keep coming, and there are always opportunities to add a new career or calling to the list.

Alternatively, your "blessing schedule" might align with some external calendars. Mother's Day and Veterans Day are obvious holidays to highlight these vocations. You might consider blessing students and educators at the beginning of the school year. You could bless retailers at the beginning of the busy Christmas shopping season, accountants during tax season, farmers during the harvest. Every local economy has its own economic schedule—its high and low seasons. You can adjust accordingly.

Finally, you might get really creative and align the callings with a specific sermon series: on healing (medicine), on creation (construction, the arts, and decorating), on justice (lawyers and police), on forgiveness (counselors), on poverty (social workers), on adoption (foster and adoptive parents), on prophecy (weather forecasters). Well, maybe not that last one.

If you are feeling overwhelmed by the possibilities and the work, we offer a number of resources and practical examples in the following chapters. Hopefully these will get your creative juices flowing.

16

Resources for Blessing

How to Interview Workers in Worship

Before you bless and commission a specific career or calling, you might wish to interview someone from that field to introduce the industry to the wider congregation. As you prepare for these interviews, remember that well-organized and thoughtfully crafted questions are key to helping workers articulate their work within God's mission. Ask thick questions that engage the worker's own personal reflection while also prompting the congregation to a deeper understanding of God's work in and through his people. Below you will find several formats with sample questions intended to fuel your imagination for what will be most impactful in your context.

Gratitude, Lament, Hope

Similar to the "creation, fall, redemption" prompt previously mentioned, ask these three basic questions:

- For what in your daily work do you give thanks to God?
- For what in your daily work do you lament?
- For what in your daily work do you hope?

Growth

This interview format focuses on the theme of growth.

- What is one beautiful thing God is growing and cultivating in you and your workplace right now?
- What is one branch that God is calling you to prune in your daily work so that something else might grow and flourish in its place?
- What are a couple seeds that you are planting in your daily work right now? We want to pray that God will nurture these seeds and cause them to both grow and produce fruit.

Trumpets, Ashes, Tears, Petitions, Fruits

This five-part prompt covers a wide range of emotions and experiences a worker might have in their daily work. It is accessible, flexible, and memorable enough to serve as a lasting framework for workers in your worship services. For additional ideas for use, see chapter 21, "Marbles and Bowls."

Trumpets of Praise
- What are some exciting things that God is doing through your work?
- How is God moving in you, your team, and your industry?

Ashes of Repentance
- What are the unique vices and temptations that are active in your particular calling or career?
- Where is there sin and injustice in your field? What might workers in your industry need to repent of?

Tears of Lament
- What in your work brings you to tears? What is broken in your industry?
- Are there moments of sadness that we can bear with you as a congregation?

Petitions
- What is one prayer/petition you are bringing to God in this current season of your work?
- How can we intercede before God on behalf of you and your industry?

Firstfruits

- What is one accomplishment from your work that we can celebrate with you as a congregation?
- What is one project or task that is unfinished that you want to give over to God in faith and trust?

Intergenerational Interviews

Broaden your definition of *worker* to include all ages and all vocations.

Questions for Children

- What is something God helped you create or complete this week at school? *(Have them bring it in and show it, or project a photo on the screen.)*
- What is your favorite thing to learn about in God's world?
- Is there something that made you sad at school—either for yourself or for someone else?

Questions for Teens and Young Adults *(Don't forget your members who are away at college. Set up a Zoom interview with them and show it during worship.)*

- Whether in school, sports, or hobbies, what is one thing you've done this year that you're truly proud of? What can we celebrate with you?
- What is one thing that is hard for you right now?
- When you think about the future, what is one thing that makes you nervous and one thing that makes you feel excited?

Questions for the Elderly

- What is God doing in and through you in this season of life?
- What are some unexpected joys about this season of life?
- How are you using this time to glorify God?
- How might we better learn and pray at your side in this season?

Adapt your prompts as needed, helping both the member and the congregation recognize that a vocational calling on one's life applies to all ages.

Visuals for Vocational Interviews and Blessings

If a picture is worth a thousand words, then visual prompts are a powerful way to enter the worker's experience. Consider having people submit photos of their workspaces, tools, and experiences. Project these images in worship as you interview and commission workers. Photos are a simple and effective way to engage people of all ages, especially youth and kids. Invite your interviewee to share about what is happening on the screen. Here are some tips:

- These workplace photos do not need to be fancy or professional. Most of us carry a perfectly adequate camera around with us. The goal isn't perfection—it's reality. Phone photos are great!
- Instead of an interview, invite the individual to share briefly about each photo. If you are concerned about time, give some specific parameters (e.g., two minutes for each photo).
- Give specific prompts. Specificity will help the worker focus on a particular aspect of their work. Instead of "Take a photo of your workstation," say, "Take a photo of what it looks like to flourish (or be frustrated) at work." Use the question prompts above to help guide the conversation.
- Keep these photos. Start a photo wall in the church or a visual mission map (see chap. 20, "Reimagining the Mission Map").
- Be mindful of privacy concerns, particularly if you're live streaming.

Vows and Charges

As mentioned in the previous chapter, vows need not be a burden for the worker. Constructed well, a series of vows will honor them and the importance of their labor. Vows help both the worker and the congregation remember that God has called, equipped, and commissioned this person for a life of service. Their verbal response acts as both an acknowledgment and assent to God's work in and through them. When writing vows, keep several things in mind:

- Vows are not meant to feel like a heavy burden that the worker must carry alone. Vows should remain hopeful, realistic, and filled with communal solidarity and assurance.

Vows and Blessing for Migrant Workers

Children of God,
The Lord of the Nations has brought you here and he has protected you through many challenges.
Even though you might be invisible to those around you, remember that the Creator sees you.
And even though you might not be able to express yourself in a new language, remember that the Creator hears you.

So go now, and extend his love through the work you do,
    embracing those who don't look like you,
    serving those who may persecute you,
    seeking justice wherever God takes you.
Keep your head high and your heart soft,
    knowing that you belong regardless of where you are.
        Because in the kingdom of the One who called you, nobody
        is a stranger.

Written by Gustavo Santos. Used with permission.

- When possible, write vows based on what you have learned from the workers themselves. Be specific to their context and their particular tasks.
- Nestle this person's vows within the larger story of God's work and ongoing activity in the world—the threefold frame of creation, fall, and redemption. God will help them. This isn't up to the worker alone. It is God's work happening in and through them, which means there is grace in abundance.
- Allow the worker to respond verbally with the words "I will" or, better yet, "I will, with God's help" or "By God's grace, I will."

Curious what these might look like? Here are a few examples.

Educators: Christ taught his disciples through stories with patience, creativity, and love. Will you strive to follow his example as you teach and train your students?
We will, with God's help.

Hospitality workers: The Lord is a gracious and generous host. At his table, our cup runs over. As you serve and host others in restaurants, hotels, and other venues throughout our city, will you strive to honor the hospitality of Christ in all you do and with all whom you serve?
We will, with God's help.

Managers and entrepreneurs: Jesus did not come to be served but to serve. As you lead your employees, ensuring fair pay and just working conditions and listening to the concerns of those entrusted to your care, will you be the hands and feet of Christ to all you meet?
We will, with God's help.

Service of Commissioning

Leader: My brothers and sisters in Christ Jesus: we are all baptized by one Spirit into one body, and given gifts for a variety of ministries for the common good. In the ministry of your daily life and work, will you proclaim by word and example the good news of God in Christ?

Answer: I will.

Leader: In your daily occupation, will you seek and serve Christ in all persons, loving your neighbor as yourself?

Answer: I will.

Leader: In the vocation to which God has called you, will you strive for justice and peace among all people, and respect the dignity of every human being?

Answer: I will.

Leader: Name the occupation for which you seek God's blessing. *(Each person names his or her occupation.)*

Let us pray.

> *Almighty God, whose Son Jesus Christ in his earthly life shared our toil and made holy our labor: be present with your people where they work. Deliver us from the service of self alone, and grant that we, remembering the account that we must one day give, may be faithful stewards of your good gifts; for the sake of him who came among us as one who serves, your Son our Savior Jesus Christ. Amen.*

In the name of God, I recognize and affirm your commitment to follow Christ in the vocation to which God has called you. May the Holy Spirit guide and strengthen you to bear faithful witness to Christ, and to carry on his work of reconciliation in the world.[1]

Commissioning

After workers have framed their calling and vowed to continue their work with God's help, they receive words of blessing reminding them that they will never do this work alone. A blessing in this context has a twofold significance: It reminds these workers of God's presence and also of the loving support of their community. Invite them forward, lay hands on them, and commission them for their particular calling or career.

A Commissioning and Charge
(incorporating the French Reformation Blessing and Num. 6:24–26)

Pastor: May the Lord bless you,

All: God goes before you to lead you.

Pastor: May the Lord keep you,

All: God goes behind you to protect you.

Pastor: May the Lord make his face shine upon you and be gracious to you,

All: God goes beneath you to support you.

Pastor: May the Lord turn his face toward you,

All: God goes above you to watch over you.

Pastor: May the Lord give you peace,

All: God goes beside you to befriend you.

Pastor: Go into God's world to serve as you have been charged.

All: Amen.

1. J. Fletcher Lowe Jr., "A Commissioning to Vocation in Daily Life," Theology of Work Project, accessed February 1, 2025, https://www.theologyofwork.org/resources/a-commissioning-to-vocation-in-daily-life. Used with permission.

Order for Commissioning to Christian Service

Dear friends, today we recognize the ministry of [name(s)] and commission [him, her, each of them] to a special task in the service of Jesus Christ.

The pastor or the person being commissioned briefly describes the form of service to which each person is being commissioned. The pastor turns the person to face the door leading out of the sanctuary. From behind, the pastor lays hands on the shoulders of the person being commissioned and invites the congregation to stretch their hands in prayer toward the person being commissioned.

_____, in the name of this congregation I commission you to this work and pledge to you our prayers, encouragement, and support. May the Holy Spirit guide and strengthen you, that in this and in all things you may do God's will in the service of Jesus Christ.

After the commissioning(s), the pastor concludes with extemporaneous prayer or with the following:

> *Almighty God, look with favor upon [name, these persons]*
> *who today (re)affirm(s) commitment to follow Christ and to serve*
>   *in his name.*
> *Give [him, her, each of them] courage, patience, and vision;*
> *and strengthen us all in our Christian vocation*
> *of witness to the world and of service to others;*
> *through Jesus Christ our Lord. Amen.*[2]

Calendar Creation

You may wish to create a schedule so that you can systematically bless and commission diverse callings and careers throughout the year. To create this calendar, you will need to know two things:

---

2. "An Order for Commissioning to Christian Service," Discipleship Ministries, United Church of Christ, accessed February 1, 2025, https://www.umcdiscipleship.org/resources/an-order-for-commissioning-to-christian-service. Original version is from "An Order for Commitment to Christian Service," altered in 2013 by the General Board of Discipleship to align with the language and rubrics used in *Services for the Ordering of Ministry in the United Methodist Church*, 2008, 2012. Used with permission.

1. Who is in your congregation?

   What sorts of workers do you have? Do you have a lot of medical professionals, construction workers, technologists? Page back to chapter 3, "Auditing Your Workers," to revisit your list.

2. What is the economic schedule of your community?

   You may wish to schedule your blessings around your community's "economic calendar." You can commission educators at the beginning of the school year, accountants at tax time, farmers at the harvest, parents on Mother's and Father's Day, and so on. National holidays? Administrative Professionals Day? Write down everything you can think of in its corresponding month, even if you have an imbalance right now. We listed several ideas to get you started.

January
- "New" workers; those who are starting new jobs, new careers, first jobs
- Janitorial staff and those in the cleaning industry

February
- Housing (realtors, mortgage brokers, construction workers)
- Truck drivers, transportation workers

March
- Landscapers (coincides with spring)
- Medical and scientific researchers (coincides with the month that COVID-19 was named a global pandemic)

April
- Accountants (coincides with tax season)
- Administrators (coincides with Administrative Professionals Day)

May
- Mothers, grandmothers (coincides with Mother's Day)
- Medical professionals (coincides with National Nurses Day)

June
- Fathers, grandfathers (coincides with Father's Day)
- Graduates

July
- Lawyers, police, and legal professionals
- Hospitality, restaurants, and travel industry

August
- Educators (coincides with the start of school)
- Farmers (coincides with the harvest)

September
- First responders

October
- Drivers and delivery workers (coincides with National Trucker Appreciation Day)
- Managers (coincides with Boss Appreciation Day)

November
- Retail employees (coincides with Christmas shopping season)
- Grocers, food service industry
- Marketing and sales

December
- Bookkeepers
- Volunteers

Even if your church doesn't write a vocational blessing for every one of these professions listed, your worship can recognize these vocations in small but impactful ways. *Even a brief mention of these workers during your prayers or preaching can be significant.*

Go back to your calendar and make some notes about how you might include these professions. If you want to help your future self, write a short prayer or blessing now in the margins. Bookmark this page in the book and plan to return to it regularly.

Get Creative

Don't forget those who are not physically in your pews on a Sunday morning. Night shift workers are home and getting a much-needed day of sleep. Some workers are clocking in just as the congregation gathers for worship. There are some who actively worship with you through the technological blessing of the live stream. As you create your vocational calendar and consider ways to bless these members and their specific callings, find creative ways to include them.

- Do a video interview ahead of time, including vows and commissioning. When you show it in worship, invite the congregation to raise a hand of blessing even though the worker is not physically present, trusting that God's blessings are not limited by space and time.
- Invite a worker to do a short, written response to several questions. This would be a perfect opportunity for the use of photographs. Feature that worker with their pictures and responses somewhere prominent for people to read. Create a wide paper frame on which members can write words of blessing and encouragement for that worker.

17

Blessing Students

August has arrived. The peace and quiet of summer worship is quickly waning. The fall ministry calendar ramping up, families returning from their final summer vacations, and the renewed presence of college students all communicate one thing: it's back-to-school time. This presents a perfect opportunity every year to bless and commission students of all ages as well as teachers, professors, and school administrators.

For a back-to-school blessing, an explanation of what students do is not necessary. Rather, your task is to wonder at the deep and profound goodness of learning within the kingdom and mission of God. We have been created with curious minds eager to explore God's world. God delights in sparkling essays, successful chemistry experiments, and classrooms that empower and enlighten. Invite students and educators to the front. Offer a few simple introductory words on the glory and goodness of learning. Don't forget your adult learners, homeschoolers, various trainers and trainees, and those who are in nontraditional educational settings. Commission and pray a blessing over their year of learning.

Educational Vows and Charges

You will need to adapt the various prayers and vows provided below based on your particular age groups and cultural contexts. University students, for example, will be able to answer and respond in a way that lower elementary students will not.

Frame Vows as a Spoken Prayer

A group of students can stand before the congregation and recite a prayer in unison, committing their school year and their learning to God. This might be beneficial for older students and those more comfortable praying and reading as a group. Consider the following prayer:

A Collect Prayer for High School and College Students

O Lord, you who promise to be with me always,
be with me this day as I begin my schoolwork;
keep me in health, I pray, and keep me from harm;
and in all that I say and do,
may I love you with all my heart, soul, mind, and strength,
and may I love my neighbor as myself,
so that I might fulfill your calling upon my life as a student.
I pray this in Christ's name. Amen.[1]

Frame Vows as an Educational Intercession

If you would prefer to frame vows as more of a prayer, you can actively petition God to work alongside students as they return to school.

Older voice: At the start of a new school year, we think of all that God is calling us to make.

Young voice: Making our lunch and making it to the bus stop on time. Making friends and making the team. Making art, music, math equations, and computer code.

All voices: God, guide us in our making.

Young voice: We think, with excitement and fear, of all the work ahead in this new school year.

1. W. David O. Taylor, *Prayers for the Pilgrimage* (InterVarsity, 2024), 115. Used with permission.

Older voice: Administration, janitorial staff, teachers, social workers, counselors, cafeteria workers, crossing guards, safety officers, classroom aides, and volunteers all work to keep our students safe, healthy, learning, and flourishing.

All voices: God, bless us in our working.

Older voice: At the start of a new school year, we pray that God will use us to share Jesus's love.

Young voice: With the friends we already have, with new kids too and even with our teachers and staff. Help us not to bully others and to stand up for those who are littler than us. Make us excited to learn about everything in the whole world, which you made and you love. Make us brave, give us wisdom, and help us to be kind.

All voices: God, use us in your world.[2]

The value of this framing is that God is the primary actor. The burden of action is less on the students and more on God. Their calling is to respond to God's work at school.

Frame Vows in a Question-and-Answer Format

While a question-and-answer format is simple in structure, it is deep in significance. It provides students of all ages the opportunity to verbally commit their school year to God, trusting that God will be with them and equip them. A simple response of "I will" or "I will, with God's help" is accessible for all ages.

Here is an example of a collective blessing and charge for parents, teachers, and students:

Charge to Parents and Caregivers

Leader: Parents and caregivers, may the Holy Spirit remind you that as covenant partners, our faith community is here for you and your children. As you send them to be molded and shaped in knowledge, may you remember they are gifts from God. Know that God's blessing is with you to help them reach their potential because they

2. Written by Meg Jenista Kuykendall. Used with permission.

are made in the image of God. As you prepare clothes, lunches, and backpacks,

People: May you be filled with peace.

Leader: As you challenge and encourage them to grow,

People: May you have perseverance and marvel at God's new work in the world.

Parents: We will, with God's help.

Charge to Educators

Leader: Educators, may God's blessing, protection, and Spirit be upon you as you guide, lead, serve, and even comfort students. You have been called by God to be ambassadors for Christ, living out God's love in your daily work. As you educate God's children of all ages,

People: May you be filled with mercy and wisdom.

Leader: As you encounter challenging situations and challenging students,

People: May you love and serve as Christ, in the strength of the Spirit.

Educators: We will, with God's help.

Charge to Students

Leader: Students, may God surround you with blessings and protection as you carry these backpacks for this new school year. As you carry notes, books, and assignments, know that you also carry the love of Christ to see everyone around you as someone loved by God.

People: May you be filled with God's grace.

Leader: As you grow in wisdom and knowledge,

People: May you grow in compassion.

Students: We will, with God's help.

Prayer and Blessing

O God, we are grateful for your created goodness. As we gather rulers, pens, crayons, notebooks, and backpacks, bless these tools to help us grow in faith and service to you and to others. Fill these backpacks with

wisdom as they are filled with books, lunches, hopes, and dreams as well
as the worries and brokenness we bring from home. May these gifts
remind our students, parents, and even us that we love them because
you first loved us. And Lord, thank you for the energy and passion of
the educators here today. Fill them with your Spirit, that they might be
wise in their preparation, strengthened in their difficult days, energized
in their moments of success, and prayerful in their daily encounters
with those with whom you have entrusted them. Bless, O God, these
students and these educators, that they might grow in grace and in the
knowledge of our Lord and Savior, Jesus Christ. Amen.[3]

Student Blessings

Similar to vows, student blessings should be adapted based on the age and
comfort level of the people you are blessing. Avoid the temptation to bring
all the cute elementary school students to the front of the sanctuary for the
congregation's sake. Of course, children are adorable and everyone loves seeing them up front. This blessing, however, is not for the adults in the room;
this blessing is *for the children*. This means it needs to be done in a way that
the children understand not only what is happening but also what is being
said. The same goes for your teens and young adults. The blessing needs to
be impactful for them. This will require some intentionality on your part.

Below is a simple template you can adapt for any age. Pick one phrase of
blessing that stays consistent throughout and fill in the alternating lines based
on the age you are blessing.

A Blessing for New Beginnings (Elementary)

As you walk onto the bus or into your school for the first time,
>   God is with you.
When you feel worried or anxious,
>   God is with you.
When you are tired from a day of learning,
>   God is with you.

---

3. Adapted from Edwin Clark, "Back to School Liturgy," Worship for Workers, accessed
July 20, 2025, https://worshipforworkers.com/resources/prayers/back-to-school-liturgy/. Used
with permission.

When you are making important decisions and you feel a weight on
    your shoulders,
    God is with you.
When you feel happy and joyful about learning more about God's world
    each day,
    God is with you.
Go now into this new beginning with blessing. You do not go alone.

A Blessing for New Beginnings (High School)

When you're looking for your locker and trying to memorize the new
    code,
    God is with you.
When you get your syllabi, textbooks, and assignment books,
    God is with you.
When it's lunchtime and you're looking around the cafeteria for a friend,
    God is with you.
When you worry about a fight with a friend or if you'll make the team
    this year,
    God is with you.
When you feel happy and excited about what this year might bring,
    God is with you.
Go now into this new beginning with blessing. You do not go alone.

Blessing the Backpacks

Many churches have started to practice a "blessing of the backpacks" before
a new school year. Students of all ages bring their backpacks into church and
wear them as they come forward for a time of prayer. Some members might
put a pin with words of encouragement on the children's backpacks. Some
have luggage tags or stickers ready to hand out.

This isn't merely a cute moment; it can also be a thick and meaningful
practice for all who are present. The backpacks are a visual reminder of the
work these students will do on a daily basis. They are called to learn, study,
memorize, and engage God's world. The backpacks can also become an embodied reminder whereby students remember this blessing every time they
throw the pack over their shoulder.

You can offer a simple prayer and blessing over the backpacks and students:

> God, bless these backpacks and those who wear them.
> May they have the tools they need to work.
> May they have the minds they need to study, hands to create, hearts to
>   serve.
> Fill them with your goodness; carry them with your strength.
> Bless them in this school year, that they may grow in grace and in the
>   knowledge of Christ.
> Amen.

If you're up to the challenge, write and lead a prayer based on the contents of a backpack:

> God, bless these backpacks and those who wear them.
> May these notebooks and computers be filled with curiosities about
>   your world.
> May the calculators show them something of your order and rightness.
> May the erasers remind them of your grace and forgiveness.
> May the contents of lunchboxes feed and nourish both body and soul.
> Bless these backpacks and those who wear them. Amen.

How might we take this August ritual and turn it into a creative year-round way of blessing the whole congregation in their daily work? Here are a few ideas to get you started.

- After "backpack Sunday," invite the adults in the congregation to bring *their* bags to church the next week—diaper bags, laptop bags, tool belts, feed bags, medical kits, lunch bags. Say a prayer and a word of blessing over all the bags and those who carry them. The children have led the way for them.
- As part of a children's message, have a couple of the adults open their bags and show the kids what is inside. Have them talk about how God equipped them that week to do their work. Have them ask the children how God was with them in their week of learning and growing. Pray together that God would continue to bless the work of their hands.

- Invite children to bring their bags back into church with special projects they made, papers they wrote, worksheets they completed. Designate an intentional space in the sanctuary where they bring their work forward during the congregational offering time and hang it up as their offering. When you say a prayer for the monetary offering, include a short prayer for the creative offering of your workers of all ages.

Get Creative

A Sunday that involves student blessings is also a unique opportunity to teach your children (and your whole congregation) a healthy theology of work. Many children might think they go to school merely because it's required of them. School is just something that they do—a necessary evil. *Coincidentally, many adults feel the same way about their daily work.* Children's books (like Richard Scarry's *What Do People Do All Day?*) are a wonderful way to creatively reimagine the importance of both study and labor in your community and the larger kingdom of God. Consider inviting your children forward and reading Richard Scarry's book to them and concluding with a prayer over them as they start their year. A few other book recommendations include *The Creator in You* by Jordan Raynor and *When God Made You* by Matthew Paul Turner.

18

Blessing Parents

She gently reads to her child
She plants the tiniest seed
She chops then she seasons the soup that is simmering
It is beautiful to me

Every spoon placed in the drawer
Every hair combed by the breeze
Every mess cleaned and mistake that's forgiven
It's beautiful to me

Slowly, slowly roots will grow to where they find water
Slowly, slowly your work is happening here

—"Your Work Is Happening Here" by The Porter's Gate

Parent prayers and blessings are often limited to Mother's Day and Father's Day. We inadvertently communicate that once a year—when the calendar dictates—we can celebrate these roles with gratitude and a well-earned day off from parenting. But outside these two secular days, the vocational work of parenting largely goes unacknowledged in many churches. We take this vocation for granted, assuming that almost everyone present just kind of "does it" on top of their other work, so a casual mention here and there in preaching or prayer will suffice.

This approach communicates that parenting is a task, not a calling.

While other people are being prayed over and talked about in terms of the call God has placed on them and the work that God equips them to do, parents, particularly those who do it full-time, find themselves wondering if their labor is, indeed, in vain. It is neither paid nor volunteer work. It has no opportunity for promotion or advancement (or even retirement!). There are no holidays or PTO. This is a job that is certainly not the same as a calling. It is simply . . . work.

The Bible says a lot about parenting. God is called Father and compared to a nursing mother (Isa. 49:15). Scripture includes parables that center on the role of parenting as one that models God's love and care for all that he created (Luke 15:11–32). And parenting takes work! Parents are to instruct and teach (Deut. 6:6–7; Eph. 6:4), guide and lead (Prov. 22:6; 29:17), and grow in the faith and love of Christ (Pss. 78; 145). More than that, parenting is not something we do *for* God as much as it is something we do *with* God. Psalm 127 compares parenting to building a house or watching over a city—if God does not build or keep watch, the workers labor in vain. If we care about labor (and if you are reading this book, our guess is that you do), we must care about parenting.

Offering vocational blessings for the work of parents not only helps the congregation better appreciate and reframe parenting as a vocation but also communicates to those who are "career parents" that their work matters to God and others. Think outside of Mother's Day and Father's Day and start blessing some parents. In some congregations, Mother's Day is already freighted with a lot of cultural and liturgical weight. You might find it wise to bless the parental calling during a month that is far removed from the secular holidays.

A Note About Pastoral Sensitivity

> Happy Mother's Day, everyone. I'd like to invite all the mothers to stand up. Let's give them a round of applause!

Many women stood. Many stayed seated. Some beamed with pride, while others tried to hold back the tears. Some women, knowing the Mother's Day drill and the pain it stirs in their hearts, simply stayed home that Sunday.

The sacred call to parenting (or lack thereof) is a complex one that requires pastoral sensitivity. On many different levels, the labor of parenting is unique in its ability to bring people to mountaintop heights and deep valleys of despair. Parenting is not just something we *do*—it's something we *are*. Of course, this is true for all vocations to some degree, but parenting is a distinct identity that is as physical as it is spiritual. When our children laugh or cry, we don't simply hear it. We *feel* it. In a vocation that is so deeply emotional and embodied, the opportunities for joy and heartbreak are tremendous.

Parenting also brings up the complex nature of familial relationships and cultural expectations. Parents become estranged from children. Parents mourn the death of a child. Parents remember the child they gave up for adoption, or they remember the other parents who gave their child life. Others long to be a parent but this dream has yet to be fulfilled.

We remind you of these complicating factors not to paralyze you or dissuade you from blessing parents—you must. This calling is too sacred, too beautiful, too incredibly hard to ignore. We say all of this simply to encourage a heightened level of pastoral care amid the complex and oftentimes painful situations experienced by those within your sanctuary. This is why we advise you not to invite all your parents to stand or come forward, thereby visibly excluding those who aren't. There are better ways to honor, bless, and (most importantly) reframe parenting as a sacred vocation. Below we offer you a variety of alternative ideas and resources to consider.

Parent Interviews

Parental interviews are a fantastic way for a congregation to explore the unique joys and challenges of raising and discipling children. Here are a few things to consider as you craft and lead these interviews.

- Publicly recognize that parenting is a holy calling in the same way as any other vocation or profession. To accomplish this, you might interview parents similar to the way you traditionally interview missionaries, workers, and the like.
- Focus on the calling of parenthood, not on the children. Asking only about caring for the kids undermines and ignores a significant portion of what many parents do.

- Avoid cute clichés or generalizations like "I bet you get sick of having dirty dishes" or "I bet you can't wait for kids to go back to school." Statements like this make blanket assumptions about parenthood that might not be true for all parents.

- Try to ask the parents God-oriented questions. Focus attention less on the parents and more on the Word, work, and power of God that are being revealed in and through the vocation of parenting. How is God showing up? What is God teaching you? How is God growing you? What do your prayers look like?

- Avoid the temptation to glorify busyness, full schedules, and exhaustion. Parenting is work and it takes a lot of effort, but like all work it was never meant to be toil.

- It may be best for the children in question not to be in the room. Can a parent truly express some of the challenges they face when the kids are in the pews? Think about the parents and the children in advance of the interview.

While standard worker questions from the previous chapters would work for parents, here are a few formats that might resonate with the experience of parenting.

Rose, Bud, Thorn

This short framework helps both the parent and the congregation think through the vocational calling of parenthood as a complex one that can have many things happening concurrently. It is not beautiful or painful. It can be both at the same time. The language also speaks to the slow and patient work of cultivation and growth.

- **Rose:** In your work of parenting, what is God calling you to blossom? Where is God's beauty showing up? How has God surprised you? What growth do you see?

- **Bud:** What is not happening yet but could in the future? What are you praying for? What are you tending in hopes that God causes it to flourish and bloom?

- **Thorn:** In your work of parenting, what thorns have emerged that are difficult to navigate and painful? When these thorns prick, what do your prayers sound like?

Write and Lead a Prayer

Being interviewed about your parenting might feel uniquely challenging given some of the dynamics we've already mentioned. Consider inviting some of your more seasoned parents to write a congregational prayer for parents. Something that speaks to the joys and challenges but also petitions God to move powerfully in and through the families of the congregation. They could lead the prayer themselves or you could do it for them. Being anonymous might allow them the space they need to speak to some of the harder and more vulnerable realities of the parental calling.

Dear Lord,
   Many days are beautiful.
   Some days are wonderful.
   There are days that are extremely difficult.
   On those days, may I believe and rest in the truth that both my chil-
      dren and I are fearfully and wonderfully made.
   I lament that unmet developmental milestones and visible traits may
      look like weaknesses to the world's eye. Lord, these feel like heavy
      burdens that must be overcome
   within our world, within our society, and sometimes within myself.
   And yet, you created us in your image,
   gifting us uniquely and filling us with your strength.
   May I embrace the way that you created me,
   and may I also embrace the way you created my children.
   Let us have faith that you will see us through our doubts and second
      guesses.
   May we hold fast to your ways and be full of courage, knowing that
      our success shouldn't be measured by how well we blend with
      others but how we stand out because of your love.
   May it be so. Amen.[1]

---

1. Written by Joanna Marsh. Used with permission.

Dislocate from the Home

To highlight the fact that parenting is a calling that goes well beyond the walls of the house, consider asking the interviewee to talk about significant places that represent the joys and challenges of parenting. Rather than vague questions about what it's like to parent, ask them to describe one physical place that represents beauty, a place of heartache, and a place of hope. You could also include the visual of three photographs that represent the three places. Here's an example of what this might look like or sound like.

- **Beauty:** The horse stables themselves are nothing beautiful to look at. I always think the horses look somewhat sad as yet another child hops on their back and pretends to be a jockey. But I have witnessed beautiful growth in the arena of this stable. In my daughter, I've seen what it is to overcome fear, chase dreams, and fall in love with something tangible—a progress from week to week that isn't always visible in the rest of parenting. . . .

- **Heartache:** Children's National Hospital presents a weird mix of beauty, heartache, and hope. I am grateful for the gift of medicine, health care, and technology. I lament the fact that as a parent I depend on them each and every day to keep my child alive. This facility partners with us to make sure the doses are right and the bloodwork is good, but the responsibility is largely on my/our shoulders to get this right. It's crushing. It's relentless. . . .

- **Hope:** My car is a place that speaks to hope. It might not feel like it every day when I'm constantly on the go, grabbing kids, picking up take-out dinner, and buckling yet another car seat. But there is a lot of laughter as we drive. Sometimes there are tears. There are honest conversations and moments of both comfortable and uncomfortable silence. I find hope in the fact that these moments as we travel are preparing us for whatever "travels" we face in the future as a family. . . .

Parent Vows and Charges

Parent vows should not feel crushing or burdensome. Given how integral parenting can be to a person's identity, be sure that these vows strongly reflect

God's presence and power working alongside them and equipping them as they go. Here are a few ideas for how to accomplish this.

Psalm 90 Adaptation

Much of the work of parenting is done with our hands—from driving a car, to preparing meals, to filling out field trip forms, to fixing the leaky sink. Psalm 90 closes with a petition from the psalmist that God would "establish the work of our hands." This short phrase acts as both a prayer and a vow. In it we recognize it is God who does the work in us and through us, but we also are charged with readying ourselves, preparing, and participating. After you have listened to your particular workers, use the following template to intersperse moments of parenting with the spoken vow "establish the work of our hands."

Psalm 90 Prayer

Leader: In all the work that we do,

Parent: Let the favor of the Lord our God be upon us!

Leader: In [making breakfast, brushing children's teeth, gathering backpacks,]

Parent: Establish the work of our hands!

Leader: In [replying to emails, running errands, reconciling siblings,]

Parent: Establish the work of our hands!

Leader: In [listening to the woes and wins of the day, washing laundry, helping with algebra,]

Parent: Establish the work of our hands!

Leader: Lord of our harvest, whatever our harvest may be, send your blessing upon it that it may be beautiful in your eyes. And since we have received the good news of Jesus, may all our work—from sowing to reaping—be rooted and built up in him and established in the faith. In the name of Jesus Christ, through the power of the Holy Spirit, we pray to you, the triune God.

Parent: Let the favor of the Lord our God be upon us! Amen.[2]

---

2. Written by Katy Kroondyk. Used with permission.

Parent and "Parents"

A church community at its best functions as a family; children walk into sanctuaries full of aunties, uncles, and parent-like figures. Of course, parents are tasked with the day-to-day work of physically raising a child, but the community is tasked with the spiritual upbringing and nurture of all its members. Consider the power of a parent vow immediately followed by a vow from the congregation to support and pray for both the parent and the child. This communicates that the parent is not alone. The community reaffirms its commitment to the spiritual care of its youngest members. All are invested in the life of these children as they grow and mature in their faith. Here's a simple example.

Leader: Parent(s), God our heavenly Father has himself equipped you for this holy calling. Will you faithfully care for all that has been entrusted to you?

Parents: We will, with God's help.

Leader: Congregation, God our heavenly Father has himself tasked you with the spiritual care of members, young and old. Will you faithfully nurture these parents and children—supporting them in prayer, teaching them to know and follow Jesus, being a Christ-like example and a spiritual companion on their faith journey?

Congregation: We will, with God's help.

Parent Blessings

Parent blessings are a wonderful opportunity to bless hands that spend a great deal of time blessing others in big and small ways. Just as the student blessings are not meant for the adults in the room, these parent blessings should be focused on the parents, not on a broader blessing for the whole family unit. If the children are in the room, it's an opportunity for them to recognize and hopefully gain a deeper appreciation for their parents' calling to this work. Here are several ideas for parent blessings.

Anointing

In some congregations this will be a familiar practice, and in others it will be new and might need some good theological framing and explanation. Anointing is a practice used throughout Scripture to signify God's blessing and call on a person's life. There is nothing magical about the oil or the physical action. It is an embodied way of reminding a worker who, and whose, they are. God has anointed them to serve, and he goes with them through the presence of the Holy Spirit. Consider a short anointing blessing like the one below.

> I anoint your hands with oil.
> With these hands, you love and serve. You care for young and old alike. You welcome others into your home and life. You tend to the sick, you bring order out of chaos. May your hands be blessed with a reminder that the God who calls you to this work blesses you and will continue to equip you with his power and love.

> I anoint your head with oil.
> With your mind, you are always looking at the bigger picture. You make plans, appointments, and playdates. You see hurts before they are spoken, you see potential before it bears fruit. You care for the physical, the emotional, the spiritual, and the material. May your mind be blessed with clarity, calm, and abundant joy. For God has marked you and claimed you as his own and promises to work in and through your mind as you serve.

Child-Led Blessings

Invite the children forward to lead a blessing for their parents. This could be done as a call and response, a fill in the blank, or just a written and spoken blessing. Consider giving the children a template like the one below. Walk them through filling it out and have them offer a blessing on their parent.

> The Lord bless you as you _____.
> The Lord keep you as you _____.
> The Lord make his face shine upon you and be gracious to you when
> _____.
>
> May the Lord turn his face toward you and give you peace. Amen.

House Blessings

House blessings have been practiced across cultures for centuries. In the early church, they were used to ward off evil spirits and pray for a boundary of spiritual protection around a home. But in more recent years, they are an embodied way to pray for God's blessing of a home and all who dwell within it. In a few chapters, you'll read more about the importance of physical space and why blessings of this nature can be deeply impactful (see chap. 22, "Blessing Workspaces"). While your congregation can't go on a field trip to walk around this person's house, there are ways to say a house blessing over a parent that can be meaningful and imaginative.

With the parent's advice, pick a few significant rooms of their house. The congregation does not need to see them to know that they exist. You could choose to project a photo if you wish. Write a short blessing over the parent's presence within that room. You aren't blessing the room; you are blessing the parent's work within that room. Here are some examples:

> May you be blessed on your front porch. As you welcome visitors, receive groceries, talk to the neighbor who stopped by to chat—may you be blessed and also be a blessing to all who come and go. May you feel safe and courageous as you step outside each day, doing the work God has set before you.

> May you be blessed in your dining room. As you gather others around your table every day, Christ the host hosts with you. As you feed people's bodies and souls, may you be fed and nourished.

The following example comes from the journal *Reformed Worship* and is used with permission. You could use this on a pastoral visit to physically bless a home. You could project a photo of the parent's house and pray this blessing for them in worship. You could also ask people to imagine their home as this prayer is spoken, trusting that the Spirit doesn't need an address book to find them.

House Blessing

> Lord Jesus Christ, there was no room for you in the inn. There is room for you here, always.

Bless the entry and all who pass through these doors.
May all who enter this home sense your peace and lovingkindness.

You are the Resurrection and the Life. You dwell with us in the most
    ordinary places.
Bless the living room, we pray.
Lord, live in us and set our hearts ablaze.

Give us our daily bread, and by your grace bring us to the great feast
    of heaven.
Bless the kitchen, we pray.
Our hearts are hungry for you, Lord.

Stay with us when evening comes, and give us strength to trust in your
    promises.
Bless the bedrooms, we pray.
Keep watch over us and help us to rest in your love.

Lord Jesus Christ, in you we are clean, and in baptism we are washed
    with water as a sign of your grace and your good promises.
Bless the bathrooms, we pray.
You have washed all our sins away and have made us whiter than snow.
    Thank you, Lord.

Let's pray the prayer Jesus taught us:
    Our Father in heaven, hallowed be your name.
    Your kingdom come, your will be done on earth as it is in heaven.
    Give us this day our daily bread,
    and forgive us our debts as we also have forgiven our debtors.
    And lead us not into temptation, but deliver us from the evil one.
    For yours is the kingdom, and the power, and the glory forever.
    Amen.

God, bless this home that in it there may be health, purity, humility,
    goodness, forgiveness, laughter, honesty, and gratitude.
May your blessing remain on this home and everyone who lives here.
We pray this in the name of the Father, the Son, and the Holy Spirit.
Amen.

Prayer for Parents and Grandparents

God,

Today we lift up those in our congregation who are parents or grandparents.

We celebrate the small and big moments that parents get to be a part of in their children's lives. From their birth and baptism to their high school graduation and wedding. It's a joy to see a child take their first steps, profess their faith in Christ, and make choices that embody your wisdom.

However, in addition to sharing in the joys of children, parents and grandparents also share in their woes. We lament for our children when they experience pain, all the more so when the parent shares responsibility for that pain. We long that all children would feel loved, and we lament that there are times when they don't.

We repent of the moments when parents let their unrealistic expectations prevent them from encouraging their children. We repent of the times when fear controls us and we don't engage in our children's pain. Help us, Lord, to see, know, and care for the children in our lives with the grace of our Father in heaven.

Give all parents your wisdom, discernment, and grace in raising their children as well as in navigating relationships with adult children. Give humility when we are confronted by our shortcomings. Give us perseverance when we feel worn out from the task you've given us.

In all these things, we acknowledge that your faithfulness extends to all generations. So, may we be active participants in passing on that faithfulness to the next generation. May we know that each diaper changed, each word of advice given, each time we embrace our children, we are faithfully living out the calling you have given us.

Bless us all as we participate in this vocation and many other vocations this coming week. In Jesus's name we pray. Amen.

Written by Travis Jamieson. Used with permission.

Collect Prayer for Workers

Almighty and ever-present God, who dwells in the unlikely places of sandwich-making and changing tables;

Convert the humble acts of this day into signposts of your coming kingdom, and recast the routines of keeping home into beautiful spaces where your kingdom grows roots;

So that freed from the burden of great things, our hearts can rest in the slow pleasures of your grace;

Through the good work of Jesus, the Son, our Lord. Amen.

Written by Phil Reinders. Used with permission.

19

Blessing Retirees

At first glance, it might seem odd to include retirement in a book on work and worship. After all, isn't retirement by definition *not working*? Isn't it a season for rest and recreation, anything but work?

It's true that the common cultural narrative assumes that when we retire, we stop working. Yet this narrative is increasingly obsolete.[1] Research shows that one in four adults over fifty expects to never retire.[2] Among those who do retire, over half plan to continue working at least part-time in retirement.[3]

But even those retired people who never return to paid employment have ample opportunities to work. Of necessity, they will do the unpaid work required for everyday living (cooking meals, taking out the trash, cultivating a

Our thanks to Rev. Dr. Mark D. Roberts for agreeing to write this chapter on our behalf. Mark has come to be a nationally recognized leader in thinking about the place of vocation and calling during the "third third of life." He was an obvious choice to fill this critical need in our book.

1. Michael McLeod, "The History of Retirement," The Fiduciary Group Investment Managers, February 26, 2021, https://www.tfginvest.com/insights/the-history-of-retirement.

2. Fatima Hussein, "About 1 in 4 US Adults 50 and Older Who Aren't Yet Retired Expect to Never Retire, AARP Study Finds," *The Hill*, April 24, 2024, https://thehill.com/homenews/ap/ap-politics/ap-more-than-1-in-4-us-adults-over-age-50-say-they-expect-to-never-retire-an-aarp-study-finds/.

3. Ryan Ermey, "Only 11% of American Workers Don't Plan to Work at All After They Retire," *CNBC*, September 6, 2024, https://www.cnbc.com/2024/09/06/survey-how-many-americans-plan-to-work-in-retirement.html.

garden, etc.). Moreover, they may choose to work as an expression of their love for God and their neighbors. They might serve meals in a local soup kitchen, lead a church mission trip, mentor a young entrepreneur, repair a neighbor's fence damaged by winds, take responsibility for their grandchildren one day a week, or care for an aging parent or spouse. Retirement becomes a time not only for rest and recreation but also for reinvesting our time and talents in new and productive ways.

Our culture's vision of what retirement should look like is not really found anywhere in Scripture. Yes, when the Levites turned fifty, they were to stop doing the hard physical labor they had done when they were younger. But the older Levites were encouraged to support their younger colleagues, perhaps as assistants or mentors (Num. 8:23–26). Work took on a new form as the Levites aged, but it didn't mutate into endless, unproductive rest.

God's first command to human beings—to be fruitful, multiply, fill the earth, subdue it, and have dominion—does not appear to have an expiration date in Scripture. According to Jesus, the Father is glorified when we bear much fruit (John 15:8). Nothing suggests this is relevant only to younger disciples. In fact, Scripture shows that God sometimes chooses people beyond our assumed retirement age of sixty-five for crucial work in the kingdom. Abram was seventy-five years old when the Lord sent him to the promised land along with his older wife, Sarai (Gen. 12:1–4). Moses was eighty when God called him to free the Israelites from Egypt (Exod. 7:7). Elizabeth was "getting on in years" when she began the work of mothering John the Baptist (Luke 1:7). Anna was eighty-four when she was chosen to announce the presence of Jesus in the temple (Luke 2:36–38). I wonder how many like Abram, Sarai, Moses, Elizabeth, and Anna are worshiping in our churches, unaware of the valuable work God has for them to do.

Certainly, God can and will use us for divine purposes as we get older. Retirement allows us to work with new freedom, creativity, and joy. Thus, we can experience the promise of Psalm 92:12–14: "The righteous will flourish like a palm tree, they will grow like a cedar in Lebanon; planted in the house of the LORD, they will flourish in the courts of our God. They will still bear fruit in old age, they will stay fresh and green."

Sadly, many who retire don't think in these terms. They've come to adopt the culture's vision of retirement as a life filled only with rest and recreation. Moreover, they are often limited by the pervasive ageism of our culture that says older people have outlived their fruitfulness.

Many worshipers—both young and old—enter the sanctuary believing that old age is not a time to bear fruit, even though Scripture makes this promise. Both young and old need a new vision of life based not on cultural bias but on biblical truth, a vision of fruitfulness for every generation that comes from being deeply rooted in God's presence.

Young and old, we all need to experience this vision expressed in the worship of our church. To be sure, the biblical understanding of lifelong fruitfulness should be preached and taught. It's worthy of study and conversation in small groups. But the biblical vision of fruitful work for all generations will dwell in our hearts through the words, prayers, songs, confessions, sacraments, offerings, blessings, and other actions of corporate worship.

What if worship leaders regularly prayed for those who are retired, that they might be fruitful in the work to which God has called them? What if, yearly, the church paused to celebrate the work of retired people, commissioning and blessing them for this crucial service?

Because this vision of fruitful work in retirement is so countercultural and therefore counterintuitive, your congregation will need biblically based instruction to fully engage in worship that affirms the potential for God-glorifying work in retirement. Such teaching will provide a theological rationale for worshipful activities that celebrate the callings of all God's people, including retired folk, to "[bear] fruit in every good work" (Col. 1:10).

Practical Possibilities for Celebrating the Work of Retired People

Including Retired People Among Workers Receiving Prayer

In this book, you've been encouraged to regularly include in worship specific prayers for various kinds of workers (managers, artists, teachers, etc.). Along with prayers for those doing paid work, you might also mention those in retirement who work for the good of the community and the city. For example, a prayer leader might say, "Lord, we ask you to bless the work of the retired people in our congregation in their service as leaders, mentors, and caregivers."

Including Retired People in Worker Testimonies

In chapter 10, you learned how to encourage workers to share their stories of God's transformative power in their various careers and callings. You can do the same thing with retired folks. If a retired member of your congregation models a countercultural fruitfulness and a life of service amid their retirement, find a way for them to share their story. This is an excellent way to challenge unbiblical cultural narratives about what retirement is for. It also encourages other retired people to glorify God through their work in this season of their lives. When prayer is offered for the retired person, others in retirement can be included in the prayers of celebration and intercession.

Commissioning Workers in Retirement

A section of the book *Work and Worship* titled "Commissioning Workers Toward Monday" offers five practical suggestions that "might prove useful in designing a commissioning service." These are testimony, affirmation, framing, vows, and blessing and charge.[4] The structure of this commissioning service can easily be adapted for those who are retired or nearing retirement.

Each year, one Sunday could be set aside for a time of blessing and commissioning for the work of retired people. Without denying the value of rest and recreation, the church needs to pause and celebrate the gifts, talents, calling, and work of those who are retired.

Plan ahead! In the weeks before the service, those participating could gather to study and discuss a biblical vision of fruitful work in retirement. They could share, encourage, and pray for one another.

Within the worship service, the time of blessing could take this form:

1. **Introduction:** The leader explains what is about to happen and why. This could be the place where biblical framing occurs (see #4 below).
2. **Testimony:** One retired person gives a short testimony, bearing witness to the potential for doing valuable, God-honoring work in retirement.
3. **Affirmation:** The leader of this service affirms those being commissioned for their desire to be fruitful during their years of retirement. They affirm that God is with them and delights in the work they do.
4. **Framing:** The leader frames work in retirement within the creative, sustaining, and redemptive work of God, emphasizing that their work is integral to the mission of God and the witness of the local church.

4. Matthew Kaemingk and Cory B. Willson, *Work and Worship: Reconnecting Our Labor and Liturgy* (Baker Academic, 2020), 247.

5. **Vows:** The leader invites those being commissioned to vow, with God's help, that they will work in retirement according to the patterns of God's good work in the world, pursuing God's kingdom, justice, and flourishing through their daily work. The leader offers thanks to God for the vows that have been made.

6. **Blessing and Charge:** The leader invites the congregation (or elders) to stand and surround those being commissioned. The leader blesses the people and the work they do in the name of the Father, Son, and Holy Spirit. The leader charges them to go out and work in ways that honor God and serve their community.

Of course, you may adapt this service for your particular context and congregation. Following the blessing and charge, the congregation might offer their glad support in the form of applause, singing, or gestures of congratulations. You may consider having some kind of reception after the service so the celebration will continue more personally and informally.

Get Creative

Retirees have important work to do within the church, blessing and guiding the next generation. Here's a tangible way to practice intergenerational ministry. Have children and teenagers all create drawings of their school, desk, or classroom. Picture the Crayola scrawls of an elementary school child next to the carefully done graphic design of a high schooler. Have each one put their name and grade on the bottom of their piece. Pin them up and invite retired members of your congregation to take one home with them. For that semester, this adult commits to praying for this child in their daily work of schooling. This practice can serve as a powerful connector for your community's disparate generations. From time to time the senior members of the congregation can come to the child and ask, "How is school going? How can I pray for you this week?"

PART 4

CREATIVE IDEAS FOR DEEPER ENGAGEMENT

20

Reimagining the Mission Map

It has become a common practice for North American churches to hang a "mission map" in their lobbies and common spaces. These maps are specifically designed to raise congregational awareness about the inspiring work of missionaries, nonprofits, church plants, and various partner ministries that the church supports globally and locally. These maps are often decorated with photos of missionaries' smiling faces, mission trips, newsletter updates, thank-you cards, and appeals for prayer and support.

The spread of the gospel around the world through the dedicated efforts of mission partners is a beautiful thing to behold, and it rightly deserves prominent attention in our churches each week. The hard work of city partners feeding the hungry, sheltering the homeless, visiting the elderly, and providing services throughout the city should be highlighted as well.

One of the reasons these global and city maps have become so ubiquitous in North American churches is because they provide a powerful visual reminder of God's activity in the local community and the world. But while these maps are potent, tangible testimonies to God's work, they also reveal a missed opportunity for the church. Who is being celebrated in these maps? Who is being excluded? What would a construction worker, a waitress, or a public defender take away from such a visual representation of God's work in the community?

Each day the construction worker goes to his worksite to ensure that families have safe, beautiful, and well-constructed houses that they can turn into homes. Each day the waitress enters the restaurant to offer citizens food, hospitality, and care amid a busy day of work. Each day the public defender stands in the courtroom to ensure that the poor and marginalized throughout the city can receive justice. Consider these three workers. Is their daily labor not a part of God's mission? Are their careers not a part of God's work in the city?

Traditional mission maps can convey an overly narrow understanding of God's mission in the world. Here God's mission includes only professional missionaries, poverty workers, and church planters. The only way a construction worker, waitress, or public defender can hope to participate in God's mission is by financially supporting the fortunate few who *actually* do God's work. To put a finer point on it, if the construction worker wishes to build a house that God truly cares about, he will need to take his hammer on a mission trip. Of course, this message is unintentional. No church would *want* their parishioners to think this way. But the message comes through subtly and powerfully all the same.

There is a simple and powerful corrective for this problem: make a new map. The visual power of the original mission map can be reimagined in a transformative way so that it incorporates every person and vocation in the church. And this isn't just hypothetical—churches around the country are already beginning to incorporate such maps into their sanctuaries.

The goal of this new map is to communicate the revolutionary and missional reality that *every follower of Jesus has a mission field.* Every disciple has a holy calling. Students, workers, parents, volunteers, and the retired are all an integral part of God's work in the city. If the "priesthood of all believers" is true, then every priest has a parish where they are called to serve. If this is a theological truth that you want your congregation to grasp intellectually, you will need a powerful visual medium by which you can reinforce it.

Below are a couple of ideas for how you might create a *vocational* mission map to highlight the powerful, diverse, and scattered work of your congregation.

Vocational Mission Map

Hang a very large map of your city in a prominent location in your church. You will honor the people's vocations by placing their work front and center (don't bury it down in a basement). Invite each member of your congregation to place a small pin on the city map where God will send them to work, serve, or study on Monday.

- You might consider incorporating this "pinning practice" directly into your worship service. Following a sermon on vocation and mission, invite your people to come forward and place a pin in the map. While they come forward, you can display photos of congregants in different workspaces around the city. This can be a powerful worship experience for your people.
- If your congregation is large, you may not have enough time during a worship service to have everyone place a pin on the map. If this is the case, you can encourage them to do this after the service. Alternatively, you can do it over a series of weeks on mission or work. Invite the schoolchildren to pin their schools one Sunday, the next week those in business, medicine, stay-at-home parents, and so on.

You can make this missional practice as simple, complex, or dynamic as you like. Below are a number of ideas you might incorporate into your local practice. Not all of these will be appropriate for your context; incorporate them as you see fit.

- Updating the map can become an annual ritual for your church. Every Labor Day Sunday, for example, the congregation can be invited to update their pins and callings. This will remind the congregation of the map's purpose and keep the map a dynamic part of congregational life.
- You might consider different colored flags to represent different sorts of callings around the city (e.g., red for medicine, blue for students, green for business, brown for volunteers, purple for parents, yellow for education).
- If you buy pins with flags, members can write their name and/or vocation on the flag before pinning it up.
- You can write a short "prayer for the pins" that is used each time a new pin goes up.
- When a worker changes jobs or retires, invite them to move their pin and say a prayer over them.

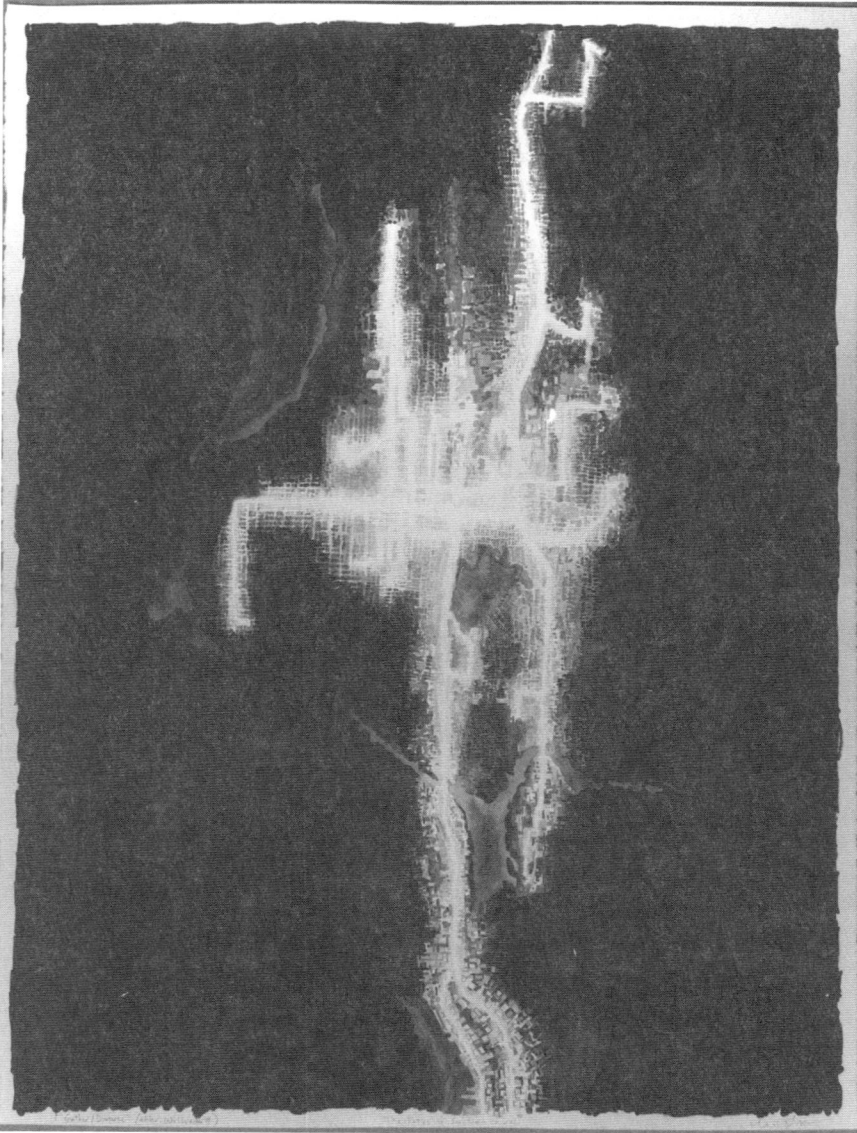

Figure 20.1. In 2016, Seattle visual artist Matthew Whitney created the following piece titled *Gather/Disperse* to visually capture the flow of congregation members as they scattered from worship to serve the Lord throughout the city. The piece served as a powerful visual reminder that the mission of God in the city is a complex and varied reality that cannot be contained by a church building or program.

- When a worker moves away, invite them to take their pin with them as a congregational gift and reminder that no matter where they are or what they are called to do, God goes with them and calls them to serve.
- Incorporate photos from workspaces into the borders of the map.
- Leave a stack of sticky notes where people can write missional prayer requests for their workplace and post them on the map.

Intergenerational Idea

- Invite kids to draw a simple map visualizing where their family members go in the city (home, school, work, ballet class, grandma's house, soccer field, etc.). Buy small refrigerator magnets in bulk and have each child take home a magnet for themselves and other members of the household. Teach a short one-sentence prayer that families and kids can use as they move their magnets to reflect their location throughout the day.

    > *God goes with me. I am never alone.*
    > *God, help me love you and love others no matter where I am.*
    > *Bless the places I go today.*

In the end, remember that this is a visual practice of reorientation. Your task is to reorient your people and their vocations toward the mission of God. Here you are trying to make a critically important shift in how they see their lives and callings to follow Jesus. This thing we call "mission" is not something for professional missionaries alone. Nor is mission something we do with our extra time and money on the weekends. It is not something that is done only in an exotic location or with a dramatic social issue. No, mission is central to our day-to-day mundane lives and work. God's mission and Spirit are present and powerful in our daily lives and callings. A vocational mission map can be an impactful asset to pastors who want to make this theological idea a missional reality.

21

Marbles and Bowls

Honestly, how do you "bring" your work to worship? Talking about all of our jobs would take forever. Praying about the minutiae of our daily lives in front of the whole church can make us feel vulnerable, selfish, and maybe even embarrassed. This is particularly true if your church is not yet accustomed to doing this. Does the whole church really want to hear about the stress of letting a colleague go on Thursday, the exhaustion of another week of sleepless nights with the baby, or the triumph of a recent promotion? Many of our deeply personal requests and laments feel off-limits.

But there is a creative new method by which churches can invite their people to carry their vocational stories, longings, and prayers forward in a way that is both public and private, both deeply meaningful and truly accessible.

A group of pastors and worship leaders in Ontario accomplished this through the creative use of marbles and bowls. As workers arrived for worship, they were invited to take several prayer marbles.[1] They carried these marbles to the front and dropped them into the appropriate bowl, saying a silent prayer.

The bowls were labeled as follows:

- **Trumpets of praise:** God, I want to celebrate what you have done this week! Thank you!

1. The original concept for the marbles and bowls, including the labels, came from Dawn Berkelaar.

- **Ashes of repentance:** God, this week I forgot you. I disobeyed. Please hear this confession and forgive me.
- **Tears of lament:** God, I don't understand what happened. Please see me in my sadness and anger.
- **Fruits of offering:** God, here is the work of my hands. You blessed me to do this and you take delight in it. I lift it up before you in gratitude and praise.
- **Petition and intercession:** God, we need you. Please act in my workplace/school/home; transform it and us.

They introduced this process over the course of several weeks so the congregation could better understand what they were doing and why (see liturgy below). They incorporated the labels for the bowls and the short prayer prompts into their worship services to help people connect their prayers for work with the common elements of worship they participate in each week. The bowls and marbles provided a tangible way to offer vocational prayers using familiar liturgical language.

As the weeks went on, workers continued to use the bowls without any pastoral prompting. A second church—also worshiping in the same building—decided that they wanted to participate as well. One week, they invited their people to share one of their "marble prayers" with another church member before dropping their marble in the bowl. Week by week, marble by marble, they used this creative prayer prompt to slowly train the people to carry their daily work and service before the Lord in worship.

Below is a straightforward way to integrate these bowls into a worship service. The full worship series—which includes these bowl litanies and much more—can be found in the journal *Reformed Worship*.[2]

The First Bowl: Trumpets of Praise

You may want to invite members of your congregation to oversee each of the bowls. Make sure to include someone who goes to school, someone who

2. Bethany Besteman, Moses Kang, and Stephanie Van Rooyen, "Work and Worship: A Seven-Week Series," *Reformed Worship* 152 (June 2024), https://reformedworship.org/issue/june-2024.

works at home, a blue-collar worker, and a retiree to indicate that every one
of us has been called by God to labor for him and for others.

> *Praiseworthy God,*
> *we want to celebrate what you have done this week,*
> *say thank you, and bring you our praises.*
> **We bring them to you.**
>
> *There have been triumphs in our work, both great and small.*
> *We thank you.*
> **We bring them to you.**

[Here the leaders can name specific experiences of work triumphs or blessings, perhaps something experienced communally.]

> *Lord, accept our prayers of praise.*
> **We bring them to you.**

The Second Bowl: Ashes of Repentance

> *God, this week we forgot you.*
> *We disobeyed. Please accept our confessions and forgive us.*
> **We bring them to you.**
> *Think back on your week of work and silently repent for when*
>   *you failed to do the work God called you to do or when you*
>   *gave less than you should have.*

[Time of silent repentance]

> *Lord, hear our prayers of repentance.*
> **We bring them to you.**

The Third Bowl: Tears of Lament

> *God, some of us don't understand what happened this week.*
> *Please see us in our sadness and anger and hear our laments.*
> **We bring them to you.**

Figure 21.1. Prayer bowls

We saw and experienced injustices in our daily lives.
How long, O Lord?
We bring them to you.

[Here the leaders can name a specific community-wide experience to lament—something in the news or in the church community itself.]

Lord, hear the cries of our hearts.
We bring them to you.

The Fourth Bowl: Fruits of Offering

To help worshipers expand and deepen their understanding of the offering, consider doing a children's message around firstfruits. Invite children to bring something to church that they made in school that week. It can be a test they did well on, a painting, a LEGO creation, whatever they want. Do a short time of show and tell. Use questions and prompts like the following to guide you.

- Some of you brought [name various items] with you today. Look at these beautiful things that you did and made this week!
- Did you work hard on this? Are you proud of what you made? Did it take a long time to make?

- Did you know that not only are *we* blessed with what you made but God is so happy with the work of your hands and your minds? God is delighted.

- A long time ago, before people gave money to the church (what we call offering), people used to come to church and bring God something they had made. It was the very best thing they made, and it was called a "firstfruit."

- Think about why it's called a "firstfruit." It's hard work to grow something. Maybe some of you like to garden. It's hard to get things to grow, but it's so exciting when it finally happens. We take delight in what we've grown. God takes delight in what you grow—in what you make at school, what you do for others, and what you build when you play.

- Some of these items you brought today might be your firstfruit. What do you think we should do with them?

- God is so happy when we offer up our firstfruits to him. We say, "Thank you, God," "We love you, God," "We give our work back to you, God."

- Today we are going to offer our firstfruits and our very own selves to God. We will do this with the work of our hands that we brought today. You can leave your work up here in front as an offering to God. You might also notice the bowl and marbles we have for our "fruits of offering." We can drop marbles in this bowl and think about what firstfruits from our week we want to offer to God. As we do these things, we can always pray to God. Let's do that now.

- Prayer: *Dear God, we give you our firstfruits. You created us to make them, and you are happy when we offer them back to you. Thank you for loving us so much that you sent Jesus to die and rise again. We want to say thank you and offer our lives and the works of our hands back to you. We love you. Amen.*

The Fifth Bowl: Petition and Intercession

God, we need you.
Please act in our workplaces, schools, and homes;
transform them and us.
We offer to you our prayers of petition and intercession.

We bring them to you.
Hear our silent prayers for our work in the week ahead.

[Silent prayers]

Lord, hear our prayers of petition and intercession.
We bring them to you.

22

Blessing Workspaces

Riding his motorcycle through the outskirts of Nairobi, an intrepid pastor makes his way into a local marketplace. He stops beside a humble clothing shop. A woman—the shop owner—is standing outside waiting expectantly for her pastor to arrive. He smiles at her and dismounts his motorcycle. He walks slowly and purposely around the store and touches the doorpost as he enters. His hand grazes over the shelves of colorful pants, socks, and shirts. He takes in the sights and the smells of the little shop. Walking through her shop, his lips move with words of blessing and prayers for protection. He sprinkles some salt here and dabs some holy water over there.

When a new business opens in Africa, it's customary for someone to place a call to the local pastor. Dutifully, they will come to bless the shop and all those who will labor therein.

We've corresponded with an innovative African ministry called Discipling Marketplace Leaders, which offered us several instructive examples of workplace blessings from across the continent. In northern Ghana, when a new piece of equipment is purchased, prayers of gratitude are offered for God's generosity as well as prayers of blessing for the productivity and usefulness of the new tool. In Togo, young apprentices are regularly blessed as they begin their training. When they complete it, a formal commissioning from the pastor is their rite of passage. When a shop or business faces economic difficulty, prayers for rescue are offered in and around Cameroonian shops.

Tanzanian pastors bless new shops but do so while reminding the business owner that they serve more than just their customers—they serve the Lord. Business owners are ultimately accountable to God for their business practices. Tanzanian pastors pray the words of Psalm 127:

> Unless the LORD builds the house,
> the builders labor in vain.
> Unless the LORD watches over the city,
> the guards stand watch in vain. (v. 1)

If you're reading this in a Western context, one that is more modern and secular, it might be difficult for you to imagine what a shop blessing might look like for your local congregation. It might seem like a completely foreign practice. Should you show up at someone's office or factory to offer a word of blessing or some drops of holy water? What do I do, anoint their laptops and smartphones with oil?

In an era of industrialization, home offices, heightened security, and suburban sprawl, many workspaces have become inaccessible—even off-limits—to pastors and prayer walks. Our modern workspaces are either too secular or too sensitive to invite your pastor in. Like a little girl in a grocery store who awkwardly runs into her kindergarten teacher, you may feel uncomfortable with the idea of meeting your pastor in your workplace. My pastor doesn't belong here. These two worlds cannot, should not, *must not* collide.

Why do these shop blessings feel awkward for so many Western Christians when they're so readily accepted in Africa? Well, many African Christians understand a theological truth that Western Christians have long forgotten—the world is an enchanted place. It is filled to the brim with spiritual forces of good and evil. As a result, the African marketplace is understood to be a space of spiritual power, presence, and contestation. Far from being invulnerable, shop owners are subject to the spiritual forces that are active in the economy. While they work, demons can attack them and angels can protect them. To the African worker, God is not a distant Father. Instead, God is an intimate friend and coworker. The Holy Spirit is alive and active in the marketplace, and these rituals acknowledge that reality. Because of their more enchanted worldview, these African pastors offer no hesitation when someone from their congregation calls them to pray over their business, shop, or field. Physically walking around a workplace and praying for protection just makes sense.

Contrary to what we might expect, these shop blessings aren't spiritually innovative or new. Four thousand years ago, the Israelites were commanded by Moses to take the words of the Lord and "write them on the doorframes of your houses and on your gates" (Deut. 6:9). This ancient Jewish practice—known as mezuzah, or "doorpost"—still exists today. If you go to Israel, you will find homes and businesses with a scroll attached to the doorpost. These scrolls remind the household whom they serve and whom they wish to honor, a reminder not only for the inhabitants but for all outsiders as well.

In medieval Europe, farmers were in constant danger of pestilence and drought. In response, priests and monks would regularly walk around their fields in ceremonies of song and prayer. These "rogation services" were conducted to comfort vulnerable farmers and petition God for protection and blessing. The priests did not stay locked up in the village church but rather walked out the doors and into the fields, praying and singing their way through the dirt and mud. The farmers were not alone. Their priest was with them.

The ancient Israelites, the medieval priests, and the African pastors all recognize something we in the modern West have forgotten. Our physical workspaces matter; they shape who we are, what we remember about God, and what we forget.

Modern Christian workers regularly decorate their desks with crosses, Bible verses, and Christian artwork. Without any pastoral direction, they set up their own little mezuzahs and ebenezers. Turning their daily commutes into a special time with God, they put sticky notes on their car dashboards and crank their worship music on the radio. One of this book's coauthors (Matthew) once received a ride from an Uber driver who reported that she would walk and pray her way around her car every morning. She said she had to do this; she needed the Lord's protection before starting her day of driving.

These physical markers and rituals have a memorial function for workers. They need to mark the space. They need a geographic reminder that this place—far from the church sanctuary—is a vibrant space of spiritual contestation, beauty, and service. It is in no way "secular."

Before we offer you some practical suggestions on how you might bless a workplace, we do need to offer a warning. We need to be clear to workers that we are not magicians or sorcerers. Our blessings do not conjure or even invite God into these workspaces. *God is already there with them.* A workplace blessing is a physical reminder of a spiritual reality: God is here and working at your side. You are not alone. Moreover, such prayers should never be framed with a "health and wealth" theology of success, one that promises that if you do all the right rituals, then God will make you rich and prosperous. Instead, these rituals remind workers that in their daily labor—their victories and successes, their struggles and failures—God is with them. With this warning clearly made, let's talk about the many benefits of these workplace blessings.

The Blessing of Workplace Blessings

Finding creative ways to bless the workspaces of your people can kick off a variety of secondary blessings. First off, this practice can give workers one more foothold for an enduring conversation with their God about their daily work. Whether a pastor performs a blessing alone or a whole group of congregation members conducts a prayer walk around a workplace, this simple practice can help your workers bridge the gap between Sunday and Monday in a concrete and memorable way. Practices like these can turn ergonomically friendly office chairs into pews and transform useful tools into handheld offerings to God. This—right here—is a place where God is at work. This—right here—is holy ground. Let's acknowledge this fact and bless this ground accordingly.

Second, this practice brings your benedictions in the sanctuary into their proper light and force. You do not bless and send your people to an anonymous place to do anonymous things. You send them to a particular location with a specific task. When they hear the words of the benediction, when they receive your blessing and charge, your people can picture their specific workspace and know that this is the place where God will meet them and work at their side. The simple act of blessing a workplace completes and perfects this closing moment of worship.

Third, *pastors* are actually blessed through this practice. Pastoral leadership can be lonely and isolating. Within the church building, the pastor's work and performance can be the center of congregational focus, examination, and even critique. Leaving the church building to bless a workspace, the pastor can breathe for a moment, celebrating and focusing on the work of another. These visitations can be profoundly encouraging, insightful, and uplifting for an exhausted pastor. Rather than isolated and lonely, they leave with a sense of deep connection and solidarity with their people.

How to Bless a Workspace

What are some tangible ways we might encourage this practice? Your own workspace is a simple and easy place to start. If you're a worship leader, take a walk around the front of your sanctuary, your desk, or the sound booth. Touch the various instruments and ask for God's blessing and guidance over all who make use of them. If you are a pastor, take a walk around your office, the pulpit, or your church building. The best place to start is with yourself.

With your congregation, you might start with some individuals who are starting a new job or a new business. You can simply ask to visit and learn more about their work. At the end of your time together, you can ask if they would like to walk with you as you pray over their labor. Rumors that you did this are likely to spread. More requests may well come. As a note, don't make your first pastoral visits to the wealthy or powerful businessmen in your congregation; start with those whose jobs might be more invisible.

Here are a few other ideas to consider:

- When a congregation member starts a new job, put out a fresh pack of sticky notes. Invite members of the church to write a word of blessing on a note. (Don't tear them off; leave the stack intact!) Then present the notes to the specific member in a worship service, praying for them and their new space. Most pads have seventy-five or one hundred notes, so their first few months of work will have one new blessing per day.
- Have members take a photo of their workspaces. Project a photo on the screen during worship and have that person respond to a few basic prompts.
  - What about this workspace do you celebrate? What gives you joy?
  - What about this workspace do you lament? What is hard and painful in this photo?
  - What do you hope happens in this workspace in the days and weeks to come?
  Listen, learn, and pray together as a community for this person and their space.
- Encourage people to write their own short prayer for their workstation. Whether it's a prayer at the kitchen sink while tackling a mountain of dishes, a prayer from the truck driver's seat while buckling up for a long day on the road, or even a prayer over a newly opened laptop—a short

prayer said at the start of each day can be a Spirit-filled way to enter a workspace with the Lord at your side.

> *God, be in my beginnings and my endings.*
> *Bless this space—the work that will happen in me and*
>   *through me.*
> *May it be for your honor and glory, that this space might*
>   *be a sacred ground*
> *where I am met with your presence and blessed with your*
>   *love.*

- Encourage your people to take a walk around their workspace. This might be a short lap around their factory, office, school, or home. It might be a stroll through the hallways or around campus. Instruct them to walk slowly and be aware of their surroundings. What do they notice? What is new? What stands out? Ask them to pray over what they see, offering it up to God and asking for his blessing.

> *God, where are you at work?*
> *God, what might you be leading me to do?*
> *God, use me. Fill me. Bless me.*

Prayer for the First Day of Work

Heavenly Father, as I embark on this new chapter of my life, I come before you with a heart filled with both excitement and trepidation.

As I step into this new workplace, may your grace surround me, opening doors of opportunity and fostering positive connections with colleagues and supervisors. Help me to approach this new environment with humility, a willingness to learn, and a spirit of cooperation.

I pray for understanding and supportive colleagues, for mentors who will guide me, and for a workplace that values collaboration and growth. May my interactions be marked by kindness, and may I be a positive influence in this new community.

Thank you, Lord, for the opportunity to embark on this new journey. I trust that you have a plan for me in this new role. Bless my efforts, and may my work be a reflection of your goodness and grace. Amen.[1]

1. Jonah McKeown, "6 Prayers for Work," *Common Good*, February 21, 2024, https://commongoodmag.com/6-prayers-for-work/. Used with permission.

Prayer of Blessing or Commissioning for Administrative Assistants and Front Desk Workers

God who ordered the universe,
We give you thanks for these
who you gift with
the skills to order our daily universes—
who make countless phone calls and write countless emails,
who organize schedules,
who receive orders,
who greet visitors,
who prepare spaces,
who create and maintain workflows,
who help keep our collective heads on straight—
for these beloved children of yours, we give you thanks.
Be with them in their work of administration.
Give them wisdom as they impact so many others.
Give them courage to trust themselves as they make difficult decisions.
Give them compassion in their multitudes of interactions—virtual
*   and face-to-face.*
May their hearts for those they serve be evident in all they do.
May their work be seen, known, and acknowledged.
May they know that theirs is a work of leadership.
May they never doubt their value.
In the name of Christ,
Amen.[2]

2. Written by Hannah Barker Nickolay. Used with permission.

23

This Time Tomorrow

This time tomorrow
With the rising of the sun, when the new light has begun to shine
This time tomorrow
May we feel your presence still, and may the love of Jesus fill our minds
Christ, you are the same
Yesterday, today

This time tomorrow
May your voice be in our ears, and may we know that you are near to us
This time tomorrow
We remember what we've learned, and may our hearts still burn with
    your love
Christ, you are the same
Yesterday, today

As the light begins to fade
May all we live and all we've made
Be worthy of your name
Be worthy of your name

This time tomorrow

—"This Time Tomorrow" by The Porter's Gate

"Where will you be at this time tomorrow?" Simple question. Deep impact.

Imagine for a moment what it might look like to ask this question of your congregation several minutes before everyone departs. *Close your eyes and visualize where you will be on Monday at 10 a.m. What will you be doing, how will you be doing it, who will you be with, and why will you be there?* The second grader thinks about being on the playground for morning recess—and she's hoping the line for the swings isn't too long. The truck driver anticipates that he'll be about 150 miles west on the freeway at that point—he wonders if the mountain pass will be clear. The landscape architect pictures her drafting table and the flower beds on the college campus that she'll be mapping out with care and creativity—she's hoping she can keep to her budget.

This simple question prompts your people to think ahead to the places where God is calling them at this time tomorrow. It reinforces the work that has just happened in the sanctuary as they head out to the community equipped to continue worshiping God through their offerings of work and daily living. The question helps them slowly begin to build that critical bridge between worship and work, the spiritual and the material, the sacred and the secular.

Our partners at Made to Flourish encourage pastors to welcome a worker onto the stage for a This Time Tomorrow (TTT) interview in which the worker has a chance to share the divine joy, heartbreak, and transformation that they are experiencing at their work. In Christian parlance, the worker is giving their testimony, bearing witness to the work of God in their daily work.

As mentioned in chapter 10, congregational testimonies are a "thick practice." They create an opportunity for workers to testify to "the power of God in the mundane." The practice builds a thicker sense of communal connection, cultivates empathy, and—most importantly—illuminates and celebrates the powerful work of God in the world. Leaders pray words of blessing over this particular worker but also invite others in the same vocational field to stand and receive a prayer of blessing over their work.

Establishing a regular TTT rhythm is an easy and simple pastoral on-ramp for those who desire worship that is more vocationally conversant. Besides worker interviews, there are numerous other ways you can engage your congregation with the TTT practice.

- Invite your congregation to pull out their phones in the sanctuary (an uncomfortable practice for some but perhaps a common practice for others). Ask them to set an alarm for tomorrow morning. When that alarm goes off, have them snap a picture of themselves inside their place of work, service, or study. Have them email these photos to the church. You can create a powerful prayer slideshow with these TTT photos. You can have this slideshow roll during a time of silent prayer, read Scripture texts over the slideshow, or even have a rolling display of the photos in the lobby under a banner that reads "Our Monday Mission." The possibilities are endless. Visuals are powerful. It is one thing to say your work and workplace matter but another thing entirely to visually witness "secular" workplaces penetrating "sacred" spaces.

- You can take TTT in a different direction if you wish. When that alarm goes off, prompt your people to pause for a brief moment of reflection.
  - At TTT, take an intentional Sabbath moment. Set aside even a few seconds to rest in God's presence. Take a deep breath, observe and give thanks for what is around you that is good and beautiful, and pray for what weighs heavy on your heart. Know that your spiritual community is doing the same in that same moment. You are not alone.
  - At TTT, say to yourself, "God goes before me to lead me, God goes behind me to protect me" (or incorporate some other words of sending that are familiar to your congregation).
- During fellowship time after church, invite people to ask TTT to each other as a way of connecting on a deeper level. Not only will people be aware of their own TTT, but they will also be prompted to remember someone else's. This fosters connection, empathy, and vocational prayer.

We have one final suggestion, and this will bring us to the conclusion of this book. Ponder for a moment: Where you will be at this time tomorrow?

We invite you, dear readers, to receive this blessing:

> Picture with me
> > where you will be tomorrow
> > what you will be doing
> > and whom you will meet.
> And pray with me
> > for the place you will be
> > for the work you've been given to do
> > and for the people you will serve.

Pause for silent prayer

May you find
    God there before you
    working alongside you
    blessing those around you.
And go in the name of the Father, the Son, and the Holy Spirit.
    Amen.[1]

1. Written by Uli Chi. Used with permission.

Worship Team Discussion Guide

If your congregation has a small team of leaders interested in working together to implement some of the lessons found within this book, we've provided a six-session discussion guide below.[1]

This guide pulls content from earlier sections and adapts it specifically for small group conversation. We've built in a high level of adaptability so you can shape these sessions according to your context and your team's time constraints. While we included only six sessions, you can easily replicate the pattern to host a conversation around rethinking the offering, a time of testimony, and other topics in this book.

Each session follows the same format:

DISCOVER
Learn and discuss the "why" of worship for workers.

CONNECT
Discuss how this idea intersects and "lands" in your own worship context.

CREATE
Dream together about new frameworks and practices for your worshiping community.

DEEPEN
Take what you've learned and created and deepen your worship for sustainable change.

1. Our deep thanks to Chris Walker for his assistance in structuring and creating this discussion guide.

REFLECT

Continue to wonder and imagine what God has done—and continues to do.

Session 1: Why Worship for Workers?

DISCOVER

Ask your worship team to read the first two chapters of this book, "Why Do We Need Worship for Workers?" and "Auditing Your Worship." Ask them to do the exercises in these chapters.

CONNECT

Invite your team to reflect on these two questions:

1. What was one new or exciting thing you read?
2. What was one thing you questioned or struggled to understand?

CREATE

Sunday   Monday

Bridging the divide between Sunday and Monday in your congregation will require a solid foundation and the building of new supports. You will also need to understand the divide that you are trying to cross.

Print out a large graphic, like the one above, with ample space to write around it. Depending on your skills, you might draw this bridge on a whiteboard or sheet of butcher paper.

1. **Strengths:** As you seek to bridge the gap, build the foundation on your strengths. Have your team write several things you and your church are

already doing well to connect worship to everyday life. What aspects of or moments in worship are facilitating a deep connection between the people and God? Write these down at the base of your bridge.

2. **Weaknesses:** What are the ways in which your worship is disconnected from everyday life? Do any of the six failures listed ring true at all? Have each member write a word or phrase that slashes across the bridge you hope to build.

3. **Opportunities:** What is the low-hanging fruit? Where will it be simple and easy to quickly deepen the connection between worship and everyday life and labor? Have each member write an idea at the top of the supports.

DEEPEN

Stay positive. Look at the strengths and opportunities you as a group have already identified. As a group, identify two or three strengths and opportunities you would like to explore further and build on. Be sure to write them down!

REFLECT

Give the group a few minutes of silence to take in what has been shared and written down on the paper.

Close with a time of reflection and sharing. How do you hope to build this bridge together? Name your questions, longings, hopes, and excitements. Write them down around the perimeter of the bridge.

Emphasize that this is a first step; nothing has to be decided or fixed today.

Session 2: Who Are Your Workers?

As a group, you are going to spend this second session discussing the callings and careers present within your congregation, mapping the diverse sorts of things that members are carrying with them from their daily lives into worship.

DISCOVER

Have your group read "Auditing Your Workers" before the meeting. As you gather, invite people to share any new thoughts that have emerged since you last met.

The first stage of bridging the chasm between Sunday and Monday is knowing who your people are, what they do, and what they carry with them into worship. In all likelihood, your worship team has never done an exercise like this before. It's possible they have never considered people's vocations and their impact on Sunday worship. This session will provide your team with an interactive and creative exercise for mapping out your congregation.

It goes without saying that "mapping" careers and callings will be easier in some scenarios than others. You will need to adapt the exercises below depending on the size of your congregation.

CONNECT

1. Hang a large piece of butcher paper on the wall. Invite everyone to take a marker and write down as many vocations, fields, and industries as they can think of represented in the church (e.g., medicine, food service, engineering, retail, police). Don't forget retirees, students, unemployed, and stay-at-home parents. It's all right if there are duplicates!

2. Take a step back and look at the paper together. Try to group the professions into several main categories. Consider using the categories in chapter 3, "Auditing Your Workers."

3. Talk about what you notice. What is new or surprising? What stands out?

CREATE

1. On another large piece of paper, write down your church's top five vocations. Spread them out so you have room to write around them.

2. Around each of these vocations, invite people to write what sorts of things people in this vocation might want to talk to God about. If you spent your life in this vocation, what might your prayers sound like? What kinds of emotions might this evoke? Are they stressed or anxious about the economy? Do they worry about patients? Are they joyful about a passing grade?

3. Talk through what you see. What themes are emerging?

DEEPEN

Take time as a team to pray over the lists of workers in front of you. This includes you! Pray for the burdens and the joys they carry with them into worship. Pray for wisdom for your team as you begin this journey to help workers worship in more authentic and honest ways.

Depending on the size of your team and the number of vocations you have listed, perhaps each person can take one of the categories and pray specifically for that group.

REFLECT

This visual exercise might have fueled your team's imagination for how to begin to deepen your worship practices for the diverse callings and careers in your congregation. You might already have a long list of things you want to implement on a Sunday morning. Remember that congregational change, particularly in worship practices, is slow and patient work. True change happens when we deepen, not expand, our practices. Expansion is implementing new ideas on a more surface level, week to week, without explanation. Deepening recognizes that true change happens in an organic way. Seeds are planted and nurtured over time, cultivated until they are ready to bloom and grow.

Cut out seed shapes on cardstock paper and send one home with each team member to help them continue reflecting on what you talked about today. Have them keep it somewhere they will see it often to remind them to pray over these vocations. If a word or phrase comes to mind, invite them to write it on the seed cutout. Remind them to bring it back for the next session.

Session 3: Gathering Workers

DISCOVER

In preparation for session three, have your group read "Workers Gather" before they arrive. Also have them bring their "seeds" with them to the meeting.

As you begin, invite your team to share one "seed" idea that has started to take root and grow in them since the last conversation. If they have not written a word or phrase on them yet, have them do so. Collect their seeds and hold on to them.

CONNECT

As a team, discuss the following questions:

1. How do we normally start our worship services?
2. Who says the first words of the day? Are they prepared or extemporaneous?

3. What do our openings communicate about our week, our worship, and God?

CREATE

Reflecting on what you've read and discussed, work together to create a rough list of things you might want your people to hear in the first two minutes of your worship service.

Work through some of the exercises in "Workers Gather."

As a team, create three or four different "gatherings" that someone could use to open your worship services. If your church doesn't normally script these words, practice leading a few of them out loud with one another.

DEEPEN

Beyond words, are there other ways to welcome people *and their daily lives* into your sanctuary?

Projection: As a group, create a visual slide to project as people walk into the sanctuary. Invite your people to prepare themselves for worship by reflecting on the events of their week. Encourage them to pause and take a deep breath, and as they breathe, lay before God all that burdens them and all that brings them joy.

Gestures: What bodily gestures might your worship leader use to welcome and prepare people for worship? Could the leader open their arms wide? Could they gesture to the table and remind the people of their primary calling to the table? Could the leader welcome the people as they pour water into the baptismal fount, reminding them of their baptismal identity? Name two or three gestures your leader might use to welcome and call the people to carry their whole selves into worship.

- TIP: Don't overdo it! Welcomes should be short and simple. Pair your words with one symbol, or one gesture, *or* one changed posture.
- TIP: Consider incorporating a short biblical text. What passage fits your welcome message? Pay particular attention to the Psalms. It's never a bad idea to saturate your worship words with Scripture!

REFLECT

Send your team home with more paper seeds. Ask them to jot down a couple of words and phrases that are on their hearts. Invite them to pray and continue reflecting on what you've created together. Remind them to bring the seeds back for the next session.

Session 4: Workers Sing

DISCOVER

In preparation for session four, have your team read "Workers Sing" before they arrive. Have them bring their "seeds" with them to the meeting. As you begin, invite your team to share what has started to take root since the last conversation. If they have not written a word or phrase on the seed, have them do so. Collect these seeds and hold on to them.

In this session, your team will be discussing the ways in which congregational singing might deepen the connections between work and worship in your community. This is a perfect opportunity to do a preliminary audit of your congregational song diet. For those who wish to do a deeper dive in the future, we highly recommend Constance Cherry's *The Music Architect*. It is transformative.

CONNECT

As a team, work through the exercise of naming your congregation's top ten songs—these might be the ten most sung (or most beloved) songs. Go through the questions that follow, contextualizing them for your team. It might be visually helpful to write this list either on a large piece of butcher paper or on a whiteboard.

CREATE

Read the section on "song framing" together and discuss the following questions:

1. How do we as a team generally frame a song?
2. Are we intentional about the words we use before and after a song?
3. How do we connect these songs to our lives in the world?

Take your top ten list and sketch out a few ways these songs might connect with the daily lives of your people. Then work together to create some framings for each song that will help deepen that connection.

You can choose to write your framings down or discuss them verbally.

DEEPEN

The deepest gift of being a worship leader is not performing. It is watching the people of God come alive carrying their praises and petitions, laments and lives before the Lord. Our sacred task is and deepest joy comes from facilitating their worship of God. When all the planning is done, we get to watch. We get to be the audience.

As you consider worship leadership, particularly around congregational singing, ask some deep and possibly difficult questions:

1. Which is more important, worship production or worship participation? Why?
2. Do I ever step away from the microphone, letting their voices be heard above my own?
3. What guides my choice in songs and the keys that I select? Am I more concerned about my performance or their participation?

Uncomfortable questions indeed. Leading worship for workers *requires* someone who will prioritize the voices and participation of the people over the voice and performance of the leader. We do not worship on behalf of the people; we facilitate their approach to the living God. Wise leaders reengage the congregation week after week, inviting them to participatory worship, an ongoing dialogue with the living God. They do not have an audience; they are the audience.

What is inhibiting you and your team from leaning into this reality? Name a few things that will need to change so that your worship team can receive the deep joy of being an audience.

REFLECT

Send home another paper seed with each team member to help them pray and continue reflecting on what you talked about today. Maybe a particular song or phrase from a song comes to mind. Invite them to write it on the seed cutout. Remind them to bring it back to the next session.

Session 5: Workers Scatter

DISCOVER

In preparation for session five, have your team read "Workers Scatter" before they arrive. Have them bring their seeds with them to the meeting. As you begin, invite your team to share what has started to take root since the last conversation. Collect these seeds and hold on to them.

In this session, you'll discuss the final moments of your worship service, both in spoken word and in song. Similar to the gathering, these final moments have a tremendous impact on how we enter the world and our work within it. Your team's mission in this session is to explore and create new ways in which you can send and scatter your people into the world with a powerful sense of blessing and purpose.

CONNECT

We recognize that in many churches the pastor offers the final words of blessing. Worship leaders, however, can still play a very important role in the sending. They can frame songs in such a way that workers are prepared for their blessing and charge. They can reorient worshipers to where God will be sending them and to the work that lies in front of them.

As a team, discuss the following questions:

1. How do we normally close our services?
2. Who says the last words of the day? Are they prepared or extemporaneous?
3. What do our closings communicate to workers?
4. List two or three of your most sung closing songs. What do they communicate about the world and our mission within it?

CREATE

Practice some new song framings and closing words of blessing and charge. Write several of these down and keep them to use in future services. Even if the end goal is leading without a script, developing the language of blessing and charge, mission and purpose, will take time and practice.

DEEPEN

Consider the role of repetition. It is not necessarily lazy or bad. It's not "slotting something in" because you ran out of good ideas or because this is simply how you've always done it. Repetition Sunday after Sunday can actually be powerfully formative. Through repetition, you are repeatedly placing meaningful words on workers' lips, songs on their hearts, and words of blessing on their souls. These words will stick with them throughout the week.

How might your closings use repetition to form workers for Monday's work? Maybe at the close of every service workers learn to open their hands and receive the blessing. Maybe they turn around and face the door during the blessing to recognize that they are being sent to a real place, with real work to do. Maybe you ask them to close their eyes and picture a person they are called to serve that week.

Your team might possibly want to use the same words or the same ritual for many weeks in a row so these words and movements sink into their souls and bones. Find creative ways to make it stick.

REFLECT

Send home another paper seed with each team member to help them pray and continue reflecting on what you talked about today. If some aspect of sending or repetition comes to mind, invite them to write it on the seed cutout. Remind them to bring it back to the next session.

Session 6: Deepening and Growing

DISCOVER

This is the final session! Whether this discussion guide has taken six weeks, six months, or a full year to complete, we hope that your team has not only grown together but also deepened their desire to lead worship for workers.

But this does not have to be the end. If your group would like to have more discussions on time for workers' testimonies, a blessing of the backpacks, or a time of celebration and commissioning for all the new retirees or graduates, by all means, feel free to continue with other sessions following a similar format.

CONNECT

Remember all the seeds you've been collecting? It's time to see what is growing. Invite your team to sit around a table together. Put the pile of seeds in the middle of the table and allow people time to look over them.

1. What do you notice about these seeds? What themes emerge?
2. How have these seeds already been growing? What has changed?

CREATE

As a team, come up with a "rose, bud, thorn" chart based on what you've experienced since you began this work. You could use a visual chart with an actual rose or you could simply discuss them. The hope is that you as a team identify the following:

Rose: What has God already done? What has God grown in and through us since we began? How has God surprised you? What blooms can we celebrate as a team?

Bud: What is still emerging for our team? What might not have happened yet but could in the future? What are we tending in hopes that God causes it to flourish and bloom?

Thorn: What might make it difficult, and what stands in the way of these buds? Where do we need buy-in from church leadership? How do we engage this work slowly and thoughtfully so as not to overwhelm ourselves and the congregation?

DEEPEN

As you close, read the following prayer. Consider returning to it frequently as you begin your rehearsals or meetings together. It serves as a reminder of two things: First, worship is slow and patient work. Wise are the leaders who allow organic growth to happen slowly. Second, there is much grace in our work of worship leadership. It's not up to us to create worship for workers on our own each week. We do so through the grace of the Son and the presence and power of the Holy Spirit.

> *It helps, now and then, to step back and take the long view. . . .*
> *We plant the seeds that one day will grow.*

*We water the seeds already planted, knowing that they hold future
     promise.*
We lay foundations that will need further development.
We provide yeast that produces effects far beyond our capabilities.
*We cannot do everything and there is a sense of liberation in
     realizing that.*
This enables us to do something and to do it well.
*It may be incomplete, but it is a beginning, a step along the way,
     an opportunity for the Lord's grace to enter and do the rest.*
*We may never see the end results, but that is the difference between
     the master builder and the worker.*
We are workers, not master builders; ministers, not messiahs.[2]

2. Ken Untener, "Prophets of a Future Not Our Own," United States Conference of Cath-olic Bishops, accessed July 20, 2025, https://www.usccb.org/prayer-and-worship/prayers-and -devotions/prayers/prophets-of-a-future-not-our-own. Used with permission.

Acknowledgments

This book would not exist without a vast network of individuals and institutions, friends and family members. Katie and Matthew's work has always depended on the gracious and generous support of a broad community of pastors and professionals, academics and artists. They have continued to encourage, educate, challenge, and inspire us in a wide variety of ways. A great cloud of witnesses contributed to every page in this book.

We begin with John Witvliet, to whom we've dedicated this book. He has been a friend, mentor, and partner for both of us for many years. His wisdom and encouragement have played a steady and constant role in our development as leaders, writers, and worshipers. While John has taught us a great deal through his scholarship and writing, his character, integrity, and leadership are what truly set him apart. Through John's selfless leadership of the Calvin Institute for Christian Worship, he and his remarkable team (to whom we also owe a heartfelt thank you) have consistently raised up a new generation of worship leaders, scholars, and artists who are ready to meet the emerging challenges and questions of a new age. John's humble desire to empower, serve, and elevate others has played an invaluable and irreplaceable role in both of our stories.

Our thanks as well to Matt Rusten, Tom Nelson, and the entire team of the Made to Flourish network. This nationwide community of pastors and churches cares deeply for workers and marketplace ministry. Their network stepped forward with an early investment in this book project, validating our sense of urgency to get resources into the hands of church leaders. Our prayer is that this book will serve the MTF network well for many years to come.

This book and the larger Worship for Workers initiative would not exist without the generous financial support of a number of foundations and institutions. Early grants and gifts from the Charis Foundation, the Calvin Institute for Christian Worship, the Brehm Center, First Presbyterian Church of Houston, and the Institute for Mission, Church, and Culture at Calvin Seminary were each absolutely critical in getting this project off the ground. We're also deeply grateful to a number of families for their continued encouragement and support: Clark and Cassie Landrum, Uli and Gayle Chi, Luke and Alyssa Davis, Tyler and Tracey Alcorn, John and Natalie McElroy, Josh and Amanda Weber, Mike and Natalie Mantel.

We're also deeply grateful for a rich network of leaders in marketplace ministries around the country who have surrounded this initiative with wisdom, creativity, and insight: Joanna Meyers and Brian Gray from the Denver Institute of Faith and Work; Malissa Mackey from Faith & Work Chicago; Paul Sohn from the Center for Faith and Work in New York; Robert Covolo from the Center for Faith and Work in Los Angeles; Jonathan Ingraham from Faith Co-op in Chattanooga; Douglas Meikle from TrueWorks Houston; David Kim from Goldenwood; Katherine Leary Alsdorf, Missy Wallace, and Lauren Gill from the Global Faith and Work Initiative; Julie Silander from the Charlotte Center for Faith and Work; and Mark Roberts from the De Pree Center.

The Porter's Gate, a collective of songwriters, worship leaders, and artists, has played an absolutely critical creative role in this effort from the very beginning. Our deep thanks to Isaac Wardell, Sandra McCracken, Leslie Jordan, Brittany Fan, Wendell Kimbrough, Paul Zach, Liz Vice, Kate Bluett, Taylor Leonhardt, Josh Garrels, Kimberly Williams, Orlando Palmer, Will McMillin, Jessica Fox, Emoni Wilkins, and Valerie and Jon Guerra.

There are many other songwriters, liturgy writers, and artists who have blessed our efforts with their creative gifts. With each resource, we learn something new about the unique beauty of worshiping communities and their diverse offerings of worship. Special thanks to our web designer, Leslie Thompson, for hearing our ideas and creating something beautiful. Know that we receive these creative gifts with gratitude.

A variety of academic colleagues have played a critical role in shaping our theological and liturgical approach to these issues of worship and work. We're particularly grateful to our colleague Cory Willson for his continued friendship, encouragement, and guidance on a number of conceptual issues that we confronted in this book. Thank you for dreaming and cocreating with us from start to finish. Your contributions are invaluable in this work. Senior colleagues who shaped our work include Nicholas Wolterstorff, Steven Garber, Constance Cherry, James K. A. Smith, Denise Daniels, Richard Mouw, Jeremy Kidwell, David Taylor, and David Rylaarsdam. Our deep thanks to colleagues for offering a number of insights into specific sections of this book: Jeremy Perigo, Ed Wilmington, Zac Hicks, Noel Snyder, Brian Hehn, Rose Wynne Brooks, and Nelson Cowan.

We've also been blessed to have a number of practicing worship leaders and pastors read sections of this book and offer critically important insights and suggestions. These include Hugh Barlett, Meg Jenista Kuykendall, Tony Howard, Mitch Penning, Steven Ottolini, Mike Farley, Dan Carter, Ben Snoek, Elizabeth Vander Haagen, Ruth Ann Schuringa, Elly Sarkany, Rachel Wilhelm, Jared Cook, and Laura DeJong. A special thanks to Chris Walker for his work in helping to develop the discussion guide. We are so grateful for your continued partnership and friendship. The fingerprints of Matthew's wife, Heather, a gifted worship director in her own right, are all over this book. Being a theologian, Matthew is long on theory and short on practice. Heather's practical theological wisdom on all things worship has consistently enriched and gently corrected him in more ways than Matthew would like to admit.

Beyond these, an array of friends and colleagues graciously agreed to read and comment on various sections of the book, including Kara Martin, Marie Blair, Rachel Collins, and Kelsey Kramer McGinnis. Last, but certainly not least, Dylan Parker, our gifted and brilliant research assistant, dedicated many hours to carefully reading, editing, and commenting on this book. His hard work getting this project across the finish line was truly invaluable.

Finally, I (Katie) am deeply grateful for a community of worshipers who have spoken into these pages with their hearts and voices. To Brian, who has been a constant source of love and support through years of ministry, both beautiful and painful. Thank you for the faithful role you've played, Sunday after Sunday, quietly supporting my calling and the work of the church. None of this would have been possible without you. To Ben, Mia, and Ava, who have grown up in the church as pastor's kids, seeing and hearing the challenges and the joys firsthand. May you see the church for all that it can and should be, and work to make it so. Thank you for asking good questions, inviting wonder and curiosity about the world, God, and everything God has made. To Fred, Kathy, Lyle, and Laurie, who embody the words of Psalm 78 and have proclaimed the praiseworthy deeds of the Lord to the next generation. Thank you for your dedication to raising us with the knowledge and love of God.

To the late Howard Vanderwell and Norma deWaal Malefyt for speaking into my calling and walking with me with their wisdom and pastoral hearts. To my mentors whose doors have always been open and whose words have been a constant source of encouragement and correction. To my Thrive colleagues who serve the church brilliantly and bravely. Finally, to the Christian Reformed Church of Washington, DC, for decades of faithful worship together. In this season and always, never forget that *your labor is not in vain.*